180 FAT-FREE LOW-FAT
DESSERTS

180 FAT-FREE LOW-FAT DESSERTS

EASY TO MAKE, DELICIOUS HEALTHY RECIPES
THE WHOLE FAMILY WILL LOVE, SHOWN
STEP-BY-STEP IN OVER 800 PHOTOGRAPHS

Wendy Doyle

southwater

This edition is published by Southwater, an imprint of Anness Publishing Ltd, Hermes House, 88–89 Blackfriars Road, London SE1 8HA; tel. 020 7401 2077; fax 020 7633 9499
www.southwaterbooks.com; www.annesspublishing.com

If you like the images in this book and would like to investigate using them for publishing, promotions or advertising, please visit our website www.practicalpictures.com for more information.

UK agent: The Manning Partnership Ltd;
tel. 01225 478444; fax 01225 478440; sales@manning-partnership.co.uk
UK distributor: Grantham Book Services Ltd;
tel. 01476 541080; fax 01476 541061; orders@gbs.tbs-ltd.co.uk
North American agent/distributor: National Book Network;
tel. 301 459 3366; fax 301 429 5746; www.nbnbooks.com
Australian agent/distributor: Pan Macmillan Australia;
tel. 1300 135 113; fax 1300 135 103; customer.service@macmillan.com.au
New Zealand agent/distributor: David Bateman Ltd; tel. (09) 415 7664; fax (09) 415 8892

Publisher: Joanna Lorenz
Managing Editor: Helen Sudell
Editor: Jenni Fleetwood
Production Controller: Ann Childers
Editorial Reader: Joy Wotton
Designer: Nigel Partridge
Recipes: Catherine Atkinson, Alex Barker, Michelle Berriedale-Johnson, Angela Boggiano, Janet Brinkworth, Carla Capalbo, Jacqueline Clark, Frances Cleary, Carol Clements, Roz Denny, Patrizia Diemling, Nicola Diggins, Joanna Farrow, Christine France, Sarah Gates, Shirly Gill, Rosamund Grant, Carole Handslip, Deh-Ta Hsiung, Shehzad Husain, Sheila Kimberley, Gilly Love, Sue Maggs, Maggie Mayhew, Maggie Parnell, Anne Sheasby, Liz Trigg, Laura Washburn, Steven Wheeler, Kate Whiteman, Elizabeth Wolf-Cohen, Jeni Wright
Photographers: William Adams-Lingwood, Karl Adamson, Edward Allwright, David Armstrong, Steve Baxter, James Duncan, Michelle Garrett, Amanda Heywood, David Jordan, Don Last, Patrick McLeavey, Michael Michaels, Thomas Odulate

ETHICAL TRADING POLICY

Because of our ongoing ecological investment programme, you, as our customer, can have the pleasure and reassurance of knowing that a tree is being cultivated on your behalf to naturally replace the materials used to make the book you are holding. For further information about this scheme, go to www.annesspublishing.com/trees

© 1999, 2008 Anness Publishing Limited

A CIP catalogue record for this book is available from the British Library.

Previously published as *Guilt-Free Desserts*

NOTES

Bracketed terms are intended for American readers.
For all recipes, quantities are given in both metric and imperial measures and, where appropriate, in standard cups and spoons.
Follow one set of measures, but not a mixture, because they are not interchangeable.
Standard spoon and cup measures are level. 1 tsp = 5ml, 1 tbsp = 15ml, 1 cup = 250ml/8fl oz.
Australian standard tablespoons are 20ml. Australian readers should use 3 tsp in place of 1 tbsp for measuring small quantities.
American pints are 16fl oz/2 cups. American readers should use 20fl oz/2.5 cups in place of 1 pint when measuring liquids.
Electric oven temperatures in this book are for conventional ovens. When using a fan oven, the temperature will probably need to be reduced by about 10–20°C/20–40°F. Since ovens vary, you should check with your manufacturer's instruction book for guidance.
Medium (US large) eggs are used unless otherwise stated.Medium (US large) eggs are used unless otherwise stated.

PUBLISHER'S NOTE

The nutritional analysis of recipes excludes all optional items and serving suggestions.

CONTENTS

INTRODUCTION

All too often, dessert is the downfall of the person trying to follow a low-fat diet. After a sensible starter and a main course composed of grilled fish or chicken and fresh vegetables, there's an almost irresistible temptation to award yourself a large portion of pudding.

The good news is that you can. You don't have to give up lovely, luscious desserts – provided you stick to the recipes in this book. Carefully designed to fit into a healthy, lighter diet, each has no more than 5g of fat per portion, and many have fewer than 200 calories.

The secret of eating for good health is making sure that your diet has a good nutritional balance. Cutting down on fat but increasing sugar is not the solution, so while these puddings bring a little sweetness into our lives, many of them do so by using small amounts of honey or the natural sugars present in fresh and dried fruits.

We all know we should be eating more fruit – it is recommended that we eat five portions of fresh fruit or vegetables each day – so fresh fruit desserts score on a variety of levels, not only supplying sweetness, but also contributing fibre, essential vitamins and minerals. These recipes make full use of the wonderfully abundant choice of fruits we now have all year round.

We are also lucky to have available lots of delicious, lighter alternatives to ingredients such as cream – so even classic rich dishes can be lightened quite easily. You'll find that, after a while, your tastes will change, and in many cases you will actually prefer the lighter, fresher flavours of low-fat desserts to some of the over-rich alternatives.

So whether you are aiming to eat less fat in order to lose weight, or just trying to eat more healthily, this book will help you do so without giving up the sweet things in life.

RIGHT: For healthy desserts, make use of the natural sweetness and colour of fruit.

FACTS ABOUT FATS

We all know we need to cut down on the amount of fat we eat – it would be difficult to live in the developed world and be unaware of that fact – but before making changes in our diet, it may be helpful to find out a bit more about the fats that we eat: some types are believed to be less harmful than others.

Fats are essential for the proper functioning of the body. However, we need the right kind of fat and the right amount. The average Western diet contains far too much of the "wrong" type of fat – saturated fat – which leads to obesity, heart problems and strokes. The daily recommended maximum amount of calories that should come from fat is between 30 and 35%. Unfortunately, many Westerners obtain well over 40% of their calories from fat, often in the form of sweet treats and desserts and pastries.

Fats in our food are made up of different types of fatty acids and glycerol. Fats may be saturated or unsaturated, with unsaturated fat further categorized as mono-unsaturated or polyunsaturated.

SATURATED FATS

To appreciate the difference between saturated and unsaturated fatty acids, it is necessary to understand a little about their molecular structure. Put very simply, fatty acids are made up of chains of carbon atoms. A common analogy is to a string of beads. Unlike beads, however, which are linked only to each other, the carbon atoms are also able to link up – or bond – with one or more other atoms. In a saturated fat, all these potential linkages have been made: the carbon atoms are linked to each other and each is further linked to two hydrogen atoms.

LEFT: A bottle of sunflower oil (left) contains mostly polyunsaturated fats (68%), while olive oil is made of up mainly mono-unsaturated fats (70%).

No further linkages are possible, and the fat is therefore said to be saturated.

Saturated fat is mainly found in foods of animal origin: meat and dairy products such as butter, which is solid at room temperature. However, there are also some saturated fats of vegetable origin, notably coconut oil and palm oil. Palm oil is the main vegetable oil used in hard margarines.

UNSATURATED FATS

Unsaturated fatty acids differ from saturated fatty acids in their structure – not all of the linkages or bonds are complete. Some of the carbon atoms are linked to only one hydrogen atom instead of the usual two, and some of the carbon atoms may be joined to each other by a double bond. Depending on how many double bonds there are, the fatty acid is described as mono-unsaturated (one double bond) or polyunsaturated (many double bonds). All the ramifications of these different molecular structures need not concern us here – suffice it to say that unsaturated fats are generally more healthy than saturated fats.

MONO-UNSATURATED FATS

These are found in foods such as olive oil, rapeseed oil, some nuts, oily fish and avocado pears. Mono-unsaturated fats are believed to be neutral, neither raising or lowering blood cholesterol levels. This, plus the fact that people in Mediterranean countries tend to have a much lower saturated fat intake as well as eating more fruit and vegetables, which are high in antioxidants, could explain why there is such a low incidence of heart disease in these countries.

ABOVE: Many common foods contain some fats. Cheese, butter, milk, cream and nuts – all of which are frequently used in desserts – should be strictly limited, unless fat free or very low fat.

POLYUNSATURATED FATS

There are two types of polyunsaturated fats. The first (omega 6) is found in vegetable and seed oils, such as sunflower or almond oil, and the second (omega 3) comes from oily fish, green leaves and some seed oils, including rapeseed or canola oil.

Polyunsaturated fats are liquid at room temperature. When vegetable oils are used in the manufacture of soft margarine, they have to be hardened artificially. During this process, the composition of some of the unsaturated fatty acids changes. In the body, these altered or "trans" fatty acids are treated like saturated fats, so, although an oil such as sunflower oil may be high in polyunsaturated fatty acids, the same is not necessarily true of a margarine made from that oil. The only way to find out is to check the label.

Polyunsaturated fats lower cholesterol levels. Although unsaturated fats are more healthy than saturated ones, most experts agree that what matters more is that we all reduce our total intake of fat.

A GUIDE TO LOW-FAT DESSERT INGREDIENTS

Watching your fat intake doesn't mean you have to forego creamy puddings. A wide range of low-fat and virtually fat-free products are on sale in supermarkets, some of them backed by alluring advertising. Clever packaging can sometimes persuade the impulse buyer to make an unwise choice, however, so always check the statistical data printed on the label.

Low-fat spreads have become very popular. These have a high water content, so, while they are perfectly acceptable for spreading on bread and teabreads, they are not necessarily suitable for cooking. When baking puddings or making cakes, look for a spread with a fat content of

around 40%. If substituting a reduced-fat spread for butter in a conventional recipe, be prepared to experiment a little, as the results will not be the same.

Try to avoid using saturated fats such as butter and hard margarine. Oils that are high in polyunsaturates, such as sunflower, corn or safflower, are the healthier option. Cakes and baked puddings made with oil are often excellent. If you must use margarine, choose a brand that is low in saturates and high in polyunsaturates.

Skimmed milk works well in batters and bakes, although you may get a better result using semi-skimmed. Yogurt and fromage frais make excellent alternatives

to cream, and when combined with honey, liqueur or other flavourings, they make delicious fillings or toppings for cheesecakes and fruit desserts. Many delectable desserts are based on soft cheeses. Cream cheese used to be the preferred option, but low-fat alternatives work just as well and are often easier to mix. If you're not familiar with it already, experiment with Quark, a virtually fat-free cheese that is very versatile.

OILS AND LOW-FAT SPREADS

CORN OIL: A polyunsaturated oil, this has a slight flavour, so it is not as good as sunflower oil for baking. Fried foods should be avoided completely if you are trying to limit your fat intake, but if you must fry this is a good choice if used sparingly, as it can reach a high temperature without smoking.
SUNFLOWER OIL SPREAD: High in polyunsaturates, this light, delicately flavoured oil is a good choice for puddings, as is safflower oil. Both can be used in cakes and bakes and are particularly good in muffins.
SUNFLOWER LIGHT SPREAD: Like reduced-fat butter, this contains about 38% fat, plus emulsified milk solids and water. The flavour is mild.
OLIVE OIL REDUCED-FAT SPREAD: With a fat content of around 63%, this spread is richer than many low-fat spreads, but it has an excellent flavour. It can be used for cooking.

LEFT: A selection of cooking oils and low-fat spreads. Always check the packaging when buying low-fat spreads – if you are going to use them for cooking, they must have a fat content of about 40%.

LOW-FAT SPREAD (rich buttermilk blend): This product is made with a high proportion of buttermilk, which is naturally low in fat. Low-fat spreads with a fat content of around 40% can be used for cooking: check the label.

VERY LOW-FAT SPREAD: This contains about 20–30% fat and has a high water content; it is not suitable for cooking.

LOW-FAT MILKS

BUTTERMILK: This is the liquid that remains after cream has been churned into butter. Buttermilk produced in this way has a light flavour, similar to skimmed milk. Commercial buttermilk is made by adding a bacterial culture to skimmed milk. This gives it a slightly sharper taste than traditional buttermilk. It is very low in fat (0.5%).

POWDERED SKIMMED MILK: This is a useful, low-fat standby. You can make up as little or as much as you need. Always follow the instructions on the packet. Of itself, the powder has quite a high fat content, so if you use too much, the drink will not be the low-fat alternative you wanted.

SEMI-SKIMMED MILK: With a fat content of only 1.6%, this milk doesn't taste as rich as full-cream milk. It is favoured by many people for everyday use for precisely this reason. Semi-skimmed milk can be used in all recipes calling for full-cream milk.

SKIMMED MILK: This milk has had virtually all the fat removed, leaving 0.1%. It is ideal for those wishing to reduce their intake of fats.

LOW-FAT CREAM SUBSTITUTES

CRÈME FRAÎCHE: Look out for half-fat versions of this thick soured cream, where the normal fat content of 40% is reduced

ABOVE: Almost all dairy products now come in low-fat or reduced-fat versions.

to 15%. Crème fraîche has a mild, lemony taste and is ideal as a topping.

GREEK YOGURT: This thick, creamy yogurt is made from whole milk with a fat content of 9.1%. A low-fat version is also available.

LOW-FAT NATURAL YOGURT: With a fat content of only about 1%, low-fat natural yogurt is a gift to the dessert cook. Use it instead of cream in whips, as a topping or as an accompaniment. Drizzle a little honey on top if you like.

LOW-FAT CHEESES

COTTAGE CHEESE: This low-fat cheese is also available in a half-fat form. Cottage cheese can be used instead of cream cheese in cheesecakes – press it through a sieve to remove the lumps.

CURD CHEESE: This low-fat soft cheese is generally made from skimmed or semi-

skimmed milk. A simple version can be made at home, using low-fat natural yogurt. Use curd cheese instead of cream cheese.

EDAM: Hard cheeses are not widely used in desserts, except in some baked cheesecakes. If a recipe does call for grated hard cheese, however, this is a good choice as it is lower in fat than standards like Cheddar or Cheshire. If you prefer the taste of Cheddar, choose a half-fat version, where the fat will be reduced to 15%.

FROMAGE FRAIS: This is a fresh, soft cheese with a very mild flavour. It is available in two grades: virtually fat-free (0.2% fat), and a more creamy variety (7.1% fat). Fromage frais is too soft to use on its own as a cheesecake filling, but it can be mixed with curd cheese.

QUARK: Perfect for many different types of pudding, this soft white cheese is virtually fat-free. It is made from fermented skimmed milk.

FAT AND CALORIE COUNTS PER 100g

The chart below lists both full-fat and low or reduced-fat typical dessert ingredients, so that
you can see the savings at a glance if you choose the healthier option.

INGREDIENT	FAT (G)	ENERGY	INGREDIENT	FAT (G)	ENERGY
OILS AND SPREADS			Curd cheese	11.7	173 Kcals/723 kJ
Butter	81.7	737 Kcals/3031 kJ	Edam	25	333 Kcals/1382 kJ
Corn oil	99.9	899 Kcals/3696 kJ	Fromage frais (plain)	7.1	113 Kcals/469 kJ
Low-fat spread	40.5	390 Kcals/1605 kJ	Half-fat Cheddar	15	261 Kcals/1091 kJ
Margarine	81.6	739 Kcals/3039 kJ	Quark	1.4	86 Kcals/360 kJ
Olive oil	99.9	899 Kcals/3696 kJ	Reduced-fat cottage cheese	1.4	78 Kcals/331 kJ
Olive oil reduced-fat spread	63	571 Kcals/2389 kJ	Very low-fat fromage frais	0.2	58 Kcals/247 kJ
Saffflower oil	99.9	899 Kcals/3696 kJ			
Sunflower oil	99.9	899 Kcals/3696 kJ	**EGGS**		
Sunflower light spread	38	357 Kcals/1494 kJ	about 2 (medium)	10.9	147 Kcals/615 kJ
Very low-fat spread	27	259 Kcals/1084 kJ	Egg white	trace	36 Kcals/153 kJ
			Egg yolk	30.5	339 Kcals/1402 kJ
MILK					
Buttermilk	0.5	37 Kcals/157 kJ	**BAKING PRODUCTS AND PRESERVES**		
Semi-skimmed milk	1.6	46 Kcals/195 kJ	Chocolate (milk)	30.3	520 Kcals/2214 kJ
Skimmed milk	0.1	33 Kcals/140 kJ	Chocolate (plain)	29.2	510 Kcals/2157 kJ
Skimmed milk powder	0.6	348 Kcals/1482 kJ	Cocoa powder	21.7	359 Kcals/1496 kJ
Whole milk	3.9	66 Kcals/275 kJ	Fatless sponge cake	6.1	294 Kcals/1230 kJ
			Honey	0	288 Kcals/1229 kJ
CREAM/CREAM SUBSTITUTES			Sugar (white)	0	394 Kcals/1648 kJ
Crème fraîche	40	380 Kcals/1582 kJ			
Double cream	48	449 Kcals/1849 kJ	**FRUIT AND NUTS**		
Greek yogurt	9.1	115 Kcals/477 kJ	Almonds	55.8	612 Kcals/2534 kJ
Half-fat crème fraîche	15	166 Kcals/692 kJ	Apples (eating)	0.1	47 Kcals/199 kJ
Low-fat yogurt (plain)	0.8	56 Kcals/236 kJ	Bananas	0.3	95 Kcals/403 kJ
Reduced-fat Greek yogurt	5.0	80 Kcals/335 kJ	Brazil nuts	68.2	682 Kcals/2813 kJ
Single cream	19.1	198 Kcals/817 kJ	Dried mixed fruit	0.4	268 Kcals/1114 kJ
Whipping cream	39.3	373 Kcals/1539 kJ	Hazelnuts	63.5	650 Kcals/2685 kJ
			Oranges	0.1	37 Kcals/158 kJ
CHEESES			Peaches	0.1	33 Kcals/142 kJ
Cheddar	34.4	412 Kcals/1708 kJ	Peanut butter (smooth)	53.7	623 Kcals/2581 kJ
Cottage cheese (plain)	3.9	98 Kcals/413 kJ	Pears	0.1	40 Kcals/169 kJ
Cream cheese	47.7	439 Kcals/1807 kJ	Pine nuts	68.6	688 Kcals/2840 kJ

Information from *The Composition of Foods* (5th edition 1991) is reproduced with the permission

of the Controller of Her Majesty's Stationery Office.

MAKING DESSERTS THE FAT-FREE WAY

To many people, dessert means lashings of cream, butter and chocolate. Nowadays, however, it is perfectly possible for a host to hoodwink guests into thinking they are having a luscious, creamy sweet, when all the while, the constituents are fat-free or low in fat.

Many ingredients are available in full-fat and reduced-fat or very low-fat forms. In every supermarket you'll find a huge array of low-fat products, such as milk, cream, yogurt, hard and soft cheeses and fromage frais, reduced-fat sweet or chocolate biscuits; low-fat, half-fat or very low-fat spreads; as well as reduced-fat ready-made desserts. Some ingredients work better than others in cooking, but often a simple substitution will spell success. In a crumb crust, for instance, reduced-fat biscuits work just as well as classic digestives.

Some of the most delicious desserts are based upon fruit. Serve fresh or dried fruit in a salad or compote, and there's absolutely no need to introduce fats. If you are making a baked or steamed pudding, or pan-frying fruit such as bananas or pineapple rings, you can get away with using the merest slick of polyunsaturated oil, especially if you use a non-stick pan. Alternatively, use spray oil: a one-second spray of sunflower oil (about 1ml) has 4.6 Kcals/18.8 kJ and just over half the fat of conventional cooking oil. Spray oil is particularly useful for lightly coating frying pans when making pancakes.

RIGHT: This sumptuous pineapple and strawberry mallow meringue looks and tastes delicious even though it is very low in fat.

When seeking inspiration for the dessert course for that special dinner party, remember that there are plenty of ingredients that naturally contain very little fat. Rice, flour, porridge oats, bread and cornflakes can all be used to make puddings and toppings, and there's no fat in wine, sherry, sugar or honey, although you may wish to restrict these for other reasons! Meringues are among the most popular puddings – topped with fresh fruit and yogurt or fromage frais, they are irresistible to eat and look great.

Spices and essences add plenty of extra flavour and colour to desserts, while decorations like rose petals, mint leaves or curls of pared citrus rind improve the appearance and stimulate the appetite.

LOW-FAT SPREADS IN COOKING
Some low-fat spreads can safely be substituted for butter or margarine in baked puddings, but others are only suitable for spreading. The limiting factor is the amount of water in the product. Very low-fat spreads achieve levels of fat of around 20% by virtue of their high water content and cannot be melted successfully. Spreads with a fat content of around 40% are suitable for spreading and for some cooking methods.

LEFT: Fresh fruit can be used to make simply superb sweet dishes, and there's no need at all to add any fat.

When using low-fat spreads for cooking, the fat may behave slightly differently to full-fat products such as butter or margarine. Be prepared to experiment a little – the results may surprise you. Some recipes actually work better with low-fat ingredients. For example, choux pastry made with half- or low-fat spread is often slightly crisper and lighter in texture than traditional choux pastry. A cheesecake biscuit base made with melted half- or low-fat spread combined with crumbs from reduced-fat biscuits may be slightly softer in texture and less crisp than one made using melted butter, but it will still be very good.

- Use heavy-based or non-stick pans – that way you won't need as much fat for cooking.
- When baking low-fat or reduced-fat cakes, it is advisable to use good quality cookware that doesn't need greasing before use, or line the pan with non-stick paper and only grease very lightly before filling.
- Look out for non-stick coated fabric sheeting. This reusable material will not stick and is amazingly versatile. It can be cut to size and used to line cake tins, baking sheets or frying pans. Heat resistant to 290°C/550°F and microwave safe, it will last for up to 5 years.
- Bake fruit in a loosely sealed parcel of greaseproof paper, moistening it

QUICK TIPS FOR FAT-FREE COOKING

with wine, fruit juice or liqueur instead of butter before sealing the parcel.
- When grilling fruit, the naturally high moisture content means that it is often unnecessary to add fat. If the fruit looks a bit dry, brush lightly and sparingly with a polyunsaturated oil such as sunflower or corn oil.
- Fruit cooked in the microwave seldom needs additional fat; add spices for extra colour and flavour.
- Poach fresh or dried fruit in natural juice or syrup – there's no need to add any fat.
- Become an expert at cooking with filo pastry. Of itself, filo is extremely low in fat, and if you brush the sheets sparingly with melted low-fat spread, it can be used to make delicious puddings that will not

significantly damage a low-fat diet and will replace other high-fat pastries.
- Avoid cooking with chocolate, which is high in fat. If you can't bear to abandon your favourite flavour, use reduced-fat cocoa powder instead.
- Get to know the full range of low- or reduced-fat products, including yogurt, crème fraîche and fromage frais. Low-fat yogurt can be used for making "creamy" sauces, but needs to be treated with a little more care than cream as it is liable to curdle when heated. Stabilize it by stirring in a little cornflour, mixed to a paste with water or skimmed milk.
- Use skimmed milk rather than whole milk in rice pudding, semolina pudding and batters.

ABOVE: Many delicious desserts can be made in moments if you have a well-stocked storecupboard.

When heating low-fat spreads, never let them get too hot. Always use a heavy-based pan over a low heat to avoid the product burning, spitting or spoiling, and stir all the time. Half-fat or low-fat spreads cannot be used for shallow- or deep-frying, traditional pastry making, rich fruit cakes, shortbread and preserves such as lemon curd.

Baked goods, such as cakes, pies and pastries, made using reduced- or low-fat spreads will not keep as well as cakes and teabreads made using butter; this is due to the lower fat content.

FRUIT PURÉES

One way of reducing the fat content of a recipe is to replace all or part of the fat with a fruit purée. This is particularly successful with breads, probably because the amount of fat is usually relatively small, and it also works well with some biscuits and bars, such as brownies.

To make a dried fruit purée for this purpose, roughly chop 115g/4oz/⅔ cup ready-to-eat dried fruit and put it in a

blender or food processor. Add 75ml/ 5 tbsp water and blend to a fairly smooth purée. Scrape into a bowl, cover and keep in the fridge for up to 3 days. When baking, simply substitute the same weight of this dried fruit purée for all or just some of the fat in the recipe. You may need to experiment a little to find the proportions that work best. If preferred, you can purée a single variety of dried fruit, such as prunes, apricots, peaches or apples, or substitute mashed fresh fruit, such as ripe bananas or lightly cooked apples. If you choose to purée fresh fruit, omit the water.

USEFUL TECHNIQUES

Delicious desserts like meringues, fruit-filled pancakes and jellies are very low
in fat. Follow the simple techniques on these pages for certain success.

WHISKING EGG WHITES

1 Place the egg whites in a completely clean, grease-free bowl. If even a speck of egg yolk is present, you will not be able to beat the whites successfully. Use one half of the shell to remove any traces of yolk.

2 Use a balloon whisk in a wide bowl for the greatest volume (egg whites can increase their volume by about eight times), but an electric hand whisk will also do an efficient job. Purists swear that eggs whisked in a copper bowl give the greatest volume.

3 Whisk the whites until they are firm enough to hold either soft or stiff peaks when you lift the whisk – see individual recipes. For stiffly whisked whites, you should be able to hold the bowl upside down without their sliding out, but this is a risky test!

MAKING PANCAKES

1 Apply a light, even coat of spray oil to a 20cm/8in pancake pan, then heat it gently. Pour in about 45ml/3 tbsp of the batter, then quickly tilt the pan so that the batter spreads to cover the bottom thinly and evenly.

2 Cook the pancake for 30-45 seconds, until it has set. Carefully lift the edge with a palette knife; the base of the pancake should have browned lightly. Shake the pan to loosen the pancake, then turn it over or flip it with a quick twist of your wrist.

3 Cook the other side of the pancake for about 30 seconds, then slide the pancake out on to a plate. Make more pancakes in the same way, then spread them with your chosen filling before rolling them or folding them neatly into triangles.

DISSOLVING GELATINE

1 Powdered gelatine is very easy to use. For every 15ml/1 tbsp of gelatine in the recipe, place 45ml/3 tbsp of very hot water in a small bowl.

2 Holding the bowl steady, sprinkle the powdered gelatine lightly and evenly over the hot liquid. Always add the gelatine to the liquid; never the other way round.

3 Stir until the gelatine has dissolved completely and the liquid is clear, with no visible crystals. You may need to stand the bowl in a pan of hot water.

UNMOULDING A JELLY

1 Have ready a serving plate that has been rinsed with cold water. Shake it but leave it damp – this will make it easier to centre the jelly. Run the tip of a knife around the moulded mixture, to loosen it.

2 Dip the mould briefly into a bowl of hot water. One or two seconds is usually enough – if you leave it for too long, the mixture will start to melt around the edges. If the jelly is stuck, dip again. Several short dips are better than one long one.

3 Quickly invert the plate over the mould. Holding mould and plate together, turn both over. Shake firmly to dislodge the jelly; as soon as you feel it drop, lift off the mould. If it does not lift off, give it another shake.

QUICK TIPS FOR GELATINE

Dissolving gelatine in cold liquid: Some recipes require gelatine to be dissolved in a cold liquid, such as apple or orange juice. In this case, pour the liquid into a small heatproof bowl and sprinkle the gelatine on top. Leave until the liquid has absorbed the gelatine and looks spongy, then place the bowl over very hot water until the gelatine has dissolved completely. You could either use a *bain marie* or simply a pan full of boiling water.

TECHNIQUES FOR TASTY TOPPINGS

Although whipped cream is taboo on a low-fat diet, there are some excellent alternatives.
Whipped "cream" can be made from skimmed milk powder or yogurt, with very good results.
Neither will hold the shape indefinitely, however, so use them as soon as possible after making.
Strained yogurt and curd cheese are simple to make at home, and tend to be lower in fat than
commercial varieties. Serve strained yogurt with puddings instead of cream, sweetening it with
a little honey, if liked. Curd cheese can be used instead of soured cream, cream cheese or butter.
Apricot glaze is very useful for brushing over a large variety of fresh fruit toppings. It gives the
fruit a lovely shiny appearance.

LOW-FAT WHIPPED "CREAM"

INGREDIENTS

2.5ml/¹/2 tsp powdered gelatine
75ml/5 tbsp water
50g/2oz/¹/4 cup skimmed milk powder
15ml/1 tbsp caster sugar
15ml/1 tbsp lemon juice

MAKES 150ML/¹/4 PINT/²/3 CUP

1 Sprinkle the powdered gelatine over
15ml/1 tbsp cold water in a small bowl
and leave to "sponge" for 5 minutes.
Place the bowl over a pan of hot water
and stir until dissolved. Leave to cool.

2 Whisk the milk powder, sugar, lemon
juice and remaining water until frothy.
Add the dissolved gelatine and whisk.
Chill for 30 minutes.

3 Using an electric hand whisk, whisk
the chilled mixture again until it holds its
shape and is very thick and frothy. Serve
within 30 minutes of making.

YOGURT PIPING CREAM

INGREDIENTS

10ml/2 tsp powdered gelatine
45ml/3 tbsp water
300ml/¹/2 pint/1¹/4 cups strained yogurt
15ml/1 tbsp fructose
2.5ml/¹/2 tsp vanilla essence
1 egg white

MAKES 450ML/³/4 PINT/SCANT 2 CUPS

1 Sprinkle the gelatine over the water in
a small bowl and leave to "sponge" for
5 minutes. Place the bowl over a
saucepan of hot water and stir until
dissolved. Leave to cool.

2 Mix together the yogurt, fructose and
vanilla essence. Stir in the gelatine. Chill
in the fridge for 30 minutes, or until just
beginning to set around the edges.

3 Whisk the egg white until stiff, then
carefully fold it into the yogurt mixture.
Spoon into a piping bag fitted with a
piping nozzle and use immediately.

STRAINED YOGURT AND SIMPLE CURD CHEESE

INGREDIENTS

600ml/1 pint/2¹/2 cups low-fat yogurt

MAKES 300ML/¹/2 PINT/1¹/4 CUPS
STRAINED YOGURT OR 115G/4OZ/
¹/2 CUP CURD CHEESE

1 For strained yogurt, line a nylon or stainless steel sieve with a double layer of muslin. Put it over a bowl and carefully pour in the low-fat yogurt.

2 Leave to drain in the fridge for 3 hours, by which time it will have separated into thick strained yogurt and watery whey. Discard the whey.

3 For curd cheese, leave to drain in the fridge for 8 hours or overnight. Spoon the curd cheese into a serving bowl, cover and keep chilled until needed.

APRICOT GLAZE

1 Place a few spoonfuls of apricot jam in a small pan and add a squeeze of lemon juice. Heat the jam, stirring until it has melted and is runny.

2 Set a wire sieve over a heatproof bowl. Pour the jam into the sieve, then stir it with a wooden spoon to help it go through the mesh.

3 Return the strained jam to the pan. Keep the glaze warm until needed, then brush it generously over the fresh fruit until evenly coated.

DECORATING WITH CITRUS RIND SHREDS

Shredded citrus rind makes a very effective decoration for a low-fat dessert. Thinly pare the rind from an orange, lemon or lime, using a swivel vegetable peeler. Take care not to remove any of the white pith, which is bitter. Cut the strips of pared rind into very fine shreds with a sharp knife. Boil the shreds for a couple of minutes in water or sugar syrup to soften them.

RIGHT: The shredded rind of oranges, lemons and limes add extra colour and appeal to this simple citrus jelly.

HOT FRUIT
PUDDINGS
AND
DESSERTS

Banish winter chills with soul-warming puddings

full of autumn's bountiful harvest of fruits, or add

spice to a summer evening's *al fresco* dinner party

with luxurious yet low-fat desserts.

SPICED PEAR AND BLUEBERRY PARCELS

**This combination makes a delicious dessert for a summer's evening and can be cooked on
a barbecue or in the oven.**

INGREDIENTS
4 firm, ripe pears
30ml/2 tbsp lemon juice
15ml/1 tbsp low-fat spread, melted
150g/5oz/1 1/4 cups blueberries
60ml/4 tbsp light muscovado sugar
freshly ground black pepper

SERVES 4

NUTRITIONAL NOTES
Per portion:

Energy	146Kcals/614kJ
Fat, total	1.8g
Saturated fat	0.37g
Cholesterol	0.2mg
Fibre	4g

2 Cut four squares of double-thickness foil, each large enough to wrap a pear and brush with melted spread. Place two pear halves on each, cut side upwards. Gather the foil around them, to hold them level.

3 Mix the blueberries and sugar together and spoon them on top of the pears. Sprinkle with black pepper. Wrap the foil over and cook for 20–25 minutes on a fairly hot barbecue or in the oven.

1 Prepare the barbecue or preheat the oven to 200°C/400°F/Gas 6. Peel the pears thinly. Cut in half lengthways. Scoop out the core from each half. Brush the pears with lemon juice, to stop them browning.

COOK'S TIP
To assemble the dessert in advance, place greaseproof paper inside the parcel, because the acid in the lemon juice may react with the foil and taint the flavour.

FRUIT AND SPICE BREAD PUDDING

—

An easy-to-make fruity dessert with a hint of spice, this is delicious served
either hot or cold.

2 Mix together the sultanas, apricots,
sugar and spice and sprinkle half the fruit
mixture over the bread in the dish.

3 Top with the remaining bread triangles
and then sprinkle over the remaining fruit.

4 Beat the eggs, milk and lemon rind
together and pour over the bread. Set
aside for about 30 minutes, to allow the
bread to absorb some of the liquid. Bake
for 45–60 minutes, until lightly set and
golden brown. Serve hot or cold.

INGREDIENTS

6 medium slices wholemeal bread
50g/2oz apricot or strawberry jam
low-fat spread, for greasing
50g/2oz/1/3 cup sultanas
50g/2oz/1/4 cup ready-to-eat dried
apricots, chopped
50g/2oz/1/3 cup soft light brown sugar
5ml/1 tsp ground mixed spice
2 eggs
600ml/1 pint/2½ cups skimmed milk
finely grated rind of 1 lemon

SERVES 4

1 Preheat the oven to 160°C/325°F/Gas 3.
Remove and discard the crusts from the
bread. Spread the bread slices with jam
and cut into small triangles. Place half
the bread triangles in a lightly greased
ovenproof dish.

NUTRITIONAL NOTES
Per portion:

Energy	305Kcals/1293kJ
Fat, total	4.51g
Saturated fat	1.27g
Cholesterol	99.3mg
Fibre	3.75g

FRUITY BREAD PUDDING

A delicious family favourite from grandmother's kitchen, with a lighter, healthier
touch for today.

NUTRITIONAL NOTES
Per portion:

Energy	190Kcals/800kJ
Fat, total	0.89g
Saturated fat	0.21g
Cholesterol	0.75mg
Fibre	1.8g

2 Remove the pan from the heat and stir in the bread cubes, spice and banana. Spoon the mixture into a shallow 1.2 litre/2 pint/5 cup ovenproof dish and pour over the milk.

3 Sprinkle with demerara sugar and bake for 25–30 minutes, until firm and golden brown. Serve hot or cold, with natural yogurt if you like.

INGREDIENTS

75g/3oz/1/2 cup mixed dried fruit
150ml/1/4 pint/2/3 cup unsweetened apple juice
115g/4oz/3–4 slices day-old brown or white bread, cubed
5ml/1 tsp mixed spice
1 large banana, sliced
150ml/1/4 pint/2/3 cup skimmed milk
15ml/1 tbsp demerara sugar
low-fat natural yogurt, to serve (optional)

SERVES 4

1 Preheat the oven to 200°C/400°F/ Gas 6. Place the dried fruit in a small pan with the apple juice and bring to the boil.

BAKED APPLES WITH RED WINE

—

Special-occasion baked apples include a delicious filling of sultanas soaked in spiced red wine.

INGREDIENTS
65g/2¹/2 oz/scant ¹/2 cup sultanas
350ml/12fl oz/1¹/2 cups red wine
pinch of grated nutmeg
pinch of ground cinnamon
50g/2oz/¹/4 cup granulated sugar
pinch of grated lemon rind
35ml/7 tsp low-fat spread
6 baking apples of even size

SERVES 6

1 Put the sultanas in a small bowl and pour over the wine. Stir in the grated nutmeg, ground cinnamon, sugar and lemon rind. Cover and leave to stand for approximately 1 hour.

2 Preheat the oven to 190°C/375°F/ Gas 5. Use a little of the low-fat spread to grease a baking dish. Core the apples, without cutting right through to the bottom.

3 Divide the sultana mixture among the apples. Spoon in a little extra spiced wine. Arrange the apples in the prepared baking dish.

4 Pour the remaining wine around the apples. Top the filling in each apple with 5ml/1 tsp of the remaining spread. Bake for 40–50 minutes, or until the apples are soft but not mushy. Serve hot or at room temperature.

NUTRITIONAL NOTES	
Per portion:	
Energy	187Kcals/784kJ
Fat, total	2.7g
Saturated fat	0.61g
Cholesterol	0.4mg
Fibre	2.6g

BAKED APPLES WITH APRICOT NUT FILLING

This is an interesting version of an old favourite. Omit the low-fat spread if you want to reduce the fat content further.

INGREDIENTS

75g/3oz/1/2 cup chopped dried apricots
20g/3/4 oz/3 tbsp chopped walnuts
5ml/1 tsp grated lemon rind
1.5ml/1/4 tsp ground cinnamon
115g/4oz/2/3 cup soft light brown sugar
30ml/2 tbsp low-fat spread
6 Bramley or other cooking apples

SERVES 6

3 Stand the apples in a baking dish just large enough to hold them comfortably side by side.

4 Melt the remaining low-fat spread and brush it over the apples. Bake for 40–45 minutes or until tender. Serve hot.

1 Preheat the oven to 190°C/375°F/ Gas 5. In a bowl, combine the apricots, walnuts, lemon rind and cinnamon. Add the sugar and rub in two-thirds of the low-fat spread until thoroughly combined.

2 Core the apples, without cutting all the way through to the base. Peel the top third of each apple. With a small knife, widen the top of each cavity by about 4cm/1 1/2 in for the filling. Spoon the filling into the apples.

NUTRITIONAL NOTES
Per portion:

Energy	263Kcals/1095kJ
Fat, total	4.9g
Saturated fat	0.89g
Cholesterol	0.3mg
Fibre	4.3g

BAKED APPLES IN HONEY AND LEMON

A classic combination of flavours in a healthy, traditional family pudding.
Serve warm, with skimmed-milk custard, if you like.

2 With a cannelle knife or a sharp knife with a narrow pointed blade, cut lines through the apple skin at intervals. Stand the apples in an ovenproof dish.

3 Mix together the honey, lemon rind, juice and low-fat spread.

INGREDIENTS
4 Bramley or other cooking apples
15ml/1 tbsp clear honey
grated rind and juice of 1 lemon
15ml/1 tbsp low-fat spread
skimmed milk custard, to serve (optional)

SERVES 4

NUTRITIONAL NOTES
Per portion:

Energy	78Kcals/326kJ
Fat, total	1.7g
Saturated fat	0.37g
Cholesterol	0.2mg
Fibre	2.4g

1 Preheat the oven to 180°C/350°F/ Gas 4. Remove the cores from the apples, taking care not to go right through the bottoms of the apples.

4 Spoon the mixture into the apples and cover the dish with foil or a lid. Bake for 40–45 minutes, or until the apples are tender. Serve with skimmed-milk custard, if you wish.

DATE, CHOCOLATE AND WALNUT PUDDING

—

Proper puddings are not totally taboo when you're reducing your fat intake –
this one is just within the rules!

2 Separate the whole egg and place the yolk in a heatproof bowl. Add the vanilla essence and sugar. Place the bowl over a pan of hot water and whisk to thicken.

3 Sift the flour and cocoa into the mixture and fold in. Stir in the milk. Whisk the egg whites and fold them in.

4 Spoon the mixture into the basin and bake for 40–45 minutes, or until the pudding has risen well and is firm to the touch. Run a knife around the pudding then turn it out and serve straight away.

INGREDIENTS

low-fat spread, for greasing
15g/¹/2 oz/1 tbsp chopped walnuts
25g/1oz/2 tbsp chopped dates
1 egg plus 1 egg white
5ml/1 tsp pure vanilla essence
30ml/2 tbsp golden caster sugar
20g/³/4 oz/3 tbsp wholemeal flour
15ml/1 tbsp cocoa powder
30ml/2 tbsp skimmed milk

SERVES 4

1 Preheat the oven to 180°C/350°F/Gas 4. Grease a 1.2 litre/2 pint/5 cup pudding basin and place a small circle of greaseproof or non-stick baking paper in the base. Spoon in the walnuts and dates.

NUTRITIONAL NOTES

Per portion:

Energy	126Kcals/530kJ
Fat, total	4.9g
Saturated fat	1.15g
Cholesterol	48.3mg
Fibre	1.3g

SULTANA AND COUSCOUS PUDDINGS

Most couscous on the market is the pre-cooked variety, which hardly needs cooking, but check
the pack instructions first. Serve hot, with skimmed-milk custard, if you like.

INGREDIENTS

50g/2oz/¹/₃ cup sultanas
475ml/16fl oz/2 cups unsweetened
apple juice
90g/3¹/₂ oz/scant 1 cup couscous
2.5ml/¹/₂ tsp mixed spice
skimmed milk custard, to serve (optional)

SERVES 4

NUTRITIONAL NOTES
Per portion:

Energy	132Kcals/557kJ
Fat, total	0.4g
Saturated fat	0.09g
Cholesterol	0mg
Fibre	0.3g

1 Lightly grease four 250ml/8fl oz/1 cup
pudding basins. Place the sultanas and
apple juice in a pan.

2 Bring the apple juice to the boil, then
lower the heat and simmer the mixture
gently for 2–3 minutes, to plump up the
fruit. Lift out about half the fruit and
place it in the bottom of the basins.

3 Add the couscous and mixed spice to
the pan and bring the liquid back to the
boil, stirring. Cover and leave over a low
heat for 8–10 minutes, or until all the
liquid has been absorbed.

4 Spoon the couscous into the basins,
spread it level, then cover the basins
tightly with foil. Place the basins in a
steamer over boiling water, cover and
steam for about 30 minutes. Run a knife
around the edges, turn the puddings out
carefully and serve straight away, with
skimmed milk custard, if you like.

COOK'S TIP
If you prefer, these puddings can be
cooked in the microwave instead of
steaming. Use individual microwave-
safe basins or teacups, cover them and
microwave on High for 8–10 minutes.

BLACKBERRY BATTER PUDDING
—

**Batter puddings are easy to make and delicious to eat. This one has a juicy
blackberry compote under a batter blanket.**

INGREDIENTS
*800g/1¾ lb/7 cups blackberries
250g/9oz/generous 1 cup
granulated sugar
45ml/3 tbsp plain flour
grated rind of 1 lemon
1.5ml/¼ tsp grated nutmeg*

FOR THE TOPPING
*225g/8oz/2 cups plain flour
225g/8oz/1 cup granulated sugar
15ml/1 tbsp baking powder
pinch of salt
250ml/8fl oz/1 cup skimmed milk
75g/3oz/6 tbsp low-fat spread, melted*

SERVES 8

1 Preheat the oven to 180°C/350°F/
Gas 4. In a large mixing bowl, combine
the blackberries with 225g/8oz/1 cup of
the sugar. Add the flour and lemon rind.
Using a large spoon, stir gently to blend.
Transfer to a 2 litre/3½ pint/8 cup
baking dish.

2 Make the topping. Sift the flour, sugar,
baking powder and salt into a large bowl.
Set aside. In a jug, combine the milk and
melted low-fat spread.

3 Gradually stir the milk mixture into the
dry ingredients and stir until the batter is
just smooth.

4 Spoon the batter over the berries. Mix
the remaining sugar with the nutmeg,
then sprinkle the mixture over the
pudding. Bake for about 50 minutes,
until the topping is set. Serve hot.

NUTRITIONAL NOTES
Per portion:

Energy	427Kcals/1812kJ
Fat, total	4.5g
Saturated fat	1g
Cholesterol	1.2mg
Fibre	4.1g

PEACH COBBLER

**All the flavour of the traditional and popular pudding,
with less fat than in a conventional cobbler.**

INGREDIENTS

*1.5kg/3–3¹/2 lb/5 cups peaches, peeled
and sliced
40g/1¹/2 oz/3 tbsp sugar
30ml/2 tbsp peach brandy
15ml/1 tbsp fresh lemon juice
15ml/1 tbsp cornflour*

FOR THE TOPPING

*115g/4oz/1 cup plain flour
7.5ml/1¹/2 tsp baking powder
1.5ml/¹/4 tsp salt
20g/³/4oz/¹/4 cup ground almonds
65g/2¹/2 oz sugar
30ml/2 tbsp low-fat spread
75ml/5 tbsp skimmed milk
1.5ml/¹/4 tsp almond essence
ice cream, to serve (optional)*

SERVES 6

1 Preheat the oven to 220°C/425°F/
Gas 7. In a bowl, toss the peaches with
the sugar, peach brandy, lemon juice and
cornflour. Spoon the peach mixture into a
2-quart baking dish.

2 Make the topping. Using a fine sieve,
sift the flour, baking powder and salt into
a mixing bowl. Stir in the ground almonds
and 50g/2oz of the sugar. With 2 knives,
or a pastry blender, cut in the spread until
the mixture resembles coarse crumbs.

3 Add the milk and almond essence and
stir until the mixture is just combined.

4 Drop the almond mixture on to the
peaches. Sprinkle with the remaining sugar.

5 Bake for 30–35 minutes until piping
hot. The cobbler topping should be
lightly browned. Serve hot, with ice
cream, if you like.

NUTRITIONAL NOTES

Per portion:

Energy	393Kcals/1661kJ
Fat, total	4.4g
Saturated fat	0.68g
Cholesterol	0.6mg
Fibre	4g

APPLE BROWN BETTY

—

A traditional favourite, this tasty dessert is good with low-fat yogurt
or fromage frais.

INGREDIENTS

50g/2oz/1 cup fresh white breadcrumbs
low-fat spread, for greasing
175g/6oz/1 cup light brown sugar
2.5ml/1/2 tsp ground cinnamon
1.5ml/1/4 tsp ground cloves
1.5ml/1/4 tsp grated nutmeg
900g/2lb eating apples
juice of 1 lemon
30ml/2 tbsp low-fat spread
20g/3/4 oz/3 tbsp finely chopped walnuts

SERVES 6

1 Preheat the grill. Spread the
breadcrumbs on a baking sheet and toast
under the grill until golden, stirring so
that they colour evenly. Set aside.

2 Preheat the oven to 190°C/375°F/Gas 5.
Grease a 2 litre/3½ pint/8 cup baking
dish. Mix the sugar with the ground
cinnamon, cloves and grated nutmeg in
a medium-sized mixing bowl.

3 Peel, core and slice the apples. Toss
the apple slices with the lemon juice to
prevent them from turning brown.

4 Sprinkle about 45ml/3 tbsp of the
breadcrumbs over the bottom of the
prepared dish. Cover with one-third of the
apples and sprinkle one-third of the
sugar-spice mixture on top.

5 Add another layer of breadcrumbs and
dot with one-quarter of the spread. Repeat
the layers two more times, ending with a
layer of breadcrumbs. Sprinkle with the
nuts, and dot with the remaining spread.

6 Bake for 35–40 minutes, until the
apples are tender and the top is golden
brown. Serve warm.

NUTRITIONAL NOTES
Per portion:

Energy	257Kcals/1073kJ
Fat, total	4.7g
Saturated fat	0.73g
Cholesterol	0.3mg
Fibre	2.9g

BLUEBERRY BUCKLE

—

**This fruity dessert is an American speciality and can be served with
low-fat Greek yogurt, if you like.**

INGREDIENTS

low-fat spread, for greasing
225g/8oz/2 cups plain flour
10ml/2 tsp baking powder
2.5ml/1/2 tsp salt
30ml/2 tbsp low-fat spread
175g/6oz/3/4 cup granulated sugar
1 egg
2.5ml/1/2 tsp pure vanilla essence
175ml/6fl oz/3/4 cup skimmed milk
450g/1lb/4 cups fresh blueberries
low-fat Greek yogurt, to serve (optional)

FOR THE TOPPING

115g/4oz/2/3 cup soft light brown sugar
50g/2oz/1/2 cup plain flour
2.5ml/1/2 tsp salt
2.5ml/1/2 tsp ground allspice
45ml/3 tbsp low-fat spread
10ml/2 tsp skimmed milk
5ml/1 tsp pure vanilla essence

SERVES 8

1 Preheat the oven to 190°C/375°F/Gas 5.
Grease a 23cm/9in round gratin dish or
shallow baking dish. Sift the flour, baking
powder and salt into a bowl. Set aside.

2 Cream the low-fat spread and the sugar.
Beat in the egg and vanilla essence. Add
the flour mixture alternately with the
milk, beginning and ending with flour.

3 Pour the mixture into the prepared dish
and sprinkle over the blueberries.

4 Make the topping. Mix the brown sugar,
flour, salt and allspice in a bowl. Rub in
the spread until the mixture resembles
coarse crumbs.

NUTRITIONAL NOTES

Per portion:

Energy	338Kcals/1432kJ
Fat, total	4.9g
Saturated fat	1.14g
Cholesterol	25.1mg
Fibre	2.1g

5 Mix the milk and vanilla essence
together. Drizzle over the flour mixture
and mix with a fork. Sprinkle the
topping over the blueberries. Bake for
45 minutes, or until a skewer inserted in
the centre comes out clean. Serve warm,
with low-fat Greek yogurt, if you like.

APPLE AND WALNUT CRUMBLE

—

**Another American favourite, combining delicious apples with crunchy walnuts,
for a simple, but tasty, dessert.**

INGREDIENTS
low-fat spread, for greasing
900g/2lb eating apples, peeled and sliced
grated rind of 1/2 lemon
15ml/1 tbsp fresh lemon juice
115g/4oz/1/2 cup light brown sugar
75g/3oz/3/4 cup plain flour
1.5ml/1/4 tsp salt
1.5ml/1/4 tsp grated nutmeg
2.5ml/1/2 tsp ground cardamom
2.5ml/1/2 tsp ground cinnamon
30ml/2 tbsp low-fat spread
20g/3/4 oz/3 tbsp walnut pieces, chopped

SERVES 6

1 Preheat the oven to 180°C/350°F/Gas 4.
Grease a 23cm/9in oval gratin dish or
shallow baking dish. Toss the apples with
the lemon rind and juice. Arrange them
evenly in the bottom of the prepared dish.

2 In a mixing bowl, combine the brown
sugar, flour, salt, nutmeg, cardamom and
cinnamon. Rub in the spread until the
mixture resembles coarse crumbs. Mix in
the walnuts.

3 With a spoon, sprinkle the walnut and
spice mixture evenly over the apples.
Cover with foil and bake for 30 minutes.

4 Remove the foil and continue baking
for about 30 minutes more, until the
apples are tender and the crumble
topping is crisp. Serve warm.

NUTRITIONAL NOTES
Per portion:

Energy	240Kcals/1003kJ
Fat, total	4.7g
Saturated fat	0.76g
Cholesterol	0.3mg
Fibre	3.1g

STRAWBERRY AND APPLE CRUMBLE

A high-fibre, low-fat version of the classic apple crumble. Fresh or frozen raspberries can be used instead of strawberries.

2 Toss together the apples, strawberries, sugar, cinnamon and orange juice. Tip the mixture into a 1.2 litre/2 pint/5 cup ovenproof dish.

3 Make the crumble. Combine the flour and oats in a bowl and mix in the low-fat spread with a fork.

4 Sprinkle the crumble evenly over the fruit. Bake for 40–45 minutes, until golden brown and bubbling. Serve warm, with low-fat custard or yogurt, if you like.

INGREDIENTS
450g/1lb cooking apples
150g/5oz/1¼ cups strawberries, hulled
30ml/2 tbsp caster sugar
2.5ml/½ tsp ground cinnamon
30ml/2 tbsp orange juice
low-fat custard or yogurt, to serve (optional)

FOR THE CRUMBLE
45ml/3 tbsp plain wholemeal flour
50g/2oz/⅔ cup porridge oats
30ml/2 tbsp low-fat spread

SERVES 4

1 Preheat the oven to 180°C/350°F/ Gas 4. Peel, core and cut the apples into approximately 5mm/¼in-size slices. Halve the strawberries.

NUTRITIONAL NOTES
Per portion:

Energy	173Kcals/729kJ
Fat, total	3.9g
Saturated fat	0.85g
Cholesterol	0.4mg
Fibre	3.5g

BLACKBERRY CHARLOTTE

—

A classic pudding, the perfect reward for an afternoon's blackberry picking.

INGREDIENTS
30ml/2 tbsp low-fat spread
175g/6oz/3 cups fresh white breadcrumbs
50g/2oz/1/3 cup soft light brown sugar
60ml/4 tbsp golden syrup
finely grated rind and juice of 2 lemons
450g/1lb cooking apples
450g/1lb/4 cups blackberries

NUTRITIONAL NOTES	
Per portion:	
Energy	346Kcals/1462kJ
Fat, total	4.2g
Saturated fat	0.74g
Cholesterol	0.5mg
Fibre	6.3g

SERVES 4

1 Preheat the oven to 180°C/350°F/Gas 4. Melt the spread in a pan with the breadcrumbs. Sauté for 5–7 minutes, until the crumbs are golden and fairly crisp. Leave to cool slightly.

2 Heat the sugar, syrup, lemon rind and juice gently in a small saucepan. Add the crumbs and mix well.

3 With a sharp knife, cut the apples in quarters, peel them and remove the cores. Slice the wedges thinly.

4 Arrange a thin layer of blackberries in a baking dish. Top with a thin layer of crumbs, then a thin layer of apple, topping the fruit with another thin layer of crumbs. Repeat the process with another layer of blackberries, followed by a layer of crumbs.

5 Continue until you have used up all the ingredients, finishing with a layer of crumbs.

6 Bake for 30 minutes, until the crumbs are golden and the fruit is soft.

COOK'S TIP
When layering the fruit and crumbs the mixture should be piled well above the top edge of the dish, because it shrinks during cooking.

CHUNKY APPLE BAKE

**This filling, economical family pudding is a good way of using up bread that is a day or so old.
The crunchy topping contrasts beautifully with the apples.**

INGREDIENTS

450g/1lb Bramley or other cooking apples
*75g/3oz wholemeal bread, about 3 slices,
without crusts*
115g/4oz/1/2 cup low-fat cottage cheese
45ml/3 tbsp light muscovado sugar
200ml/7fl oz/scant 1 cup skimmed milk
5ml/1 tsp demerara sugar

SERVES 4

1 Preheat the oven to 220°C/425°F/Gas 7.
Peel the apples, cut them in quarters and
remove the cores.

VARIATION

You could experiment with other types
of bread such as oat, rye or white.
Pears could be used instead of apples.

NUTRITIONAL NOTES
Per portion:

Energy	158Kcals/669kJ
Fat, total	1g
Saturated fat	0.38g
Cholesterol	2.4mg
Fibre	2.3g

2 Using a sharp knife, roughly chop the
apples into even-size pieces, about
1cm/1/2 in in width and depth.

3 Cut the bread into 1cm/1/2 in cubes. Do
not use crusts as these will be too thick
for the mixture.

4 Put the apples in a bowl and add the
bread cubes, cottage cheese and
muscovado sugar. Toss lightly to mix.

5 Stir in the skimmed milk and then tip
the mixture into a wide ovenproof dish.
Sprinkle demerara sugar over the top of
the mixture.

6 Bake for 30–35 minutes, or until the
apple bake is golden brown and bubbling.
Serve hot.

COOK'S TIP

You may need to adjust the amount of
milk used, depending on the dryness of
the bread; the more stale the bread, the
more milk it will absorb. The texture
should be very moist but not
falling apart.

APPLE COUSCOUS PUDDING
—

This unusual mixture makes a delicious family pudding with a rich fruity flavour, but virtually no fat.

INGREDIENTS
600ml/1 pint/2½ cups unsweetened apple juice
115g/4oz/⅔ cup couscous
40g/1½oz/¼ cup sultanas
2.5ml/½ tsp mixed spice
2 large Bramley or other cooking apples
30ml/2 tbsp demerara sugar
low-fat natural yogurt, to serve

SERVES 4

NUTRITIONAL NOTES
Per portion:

Energy	194Kcals/815kJ
Fat, total	0.58g
Saturated fat	0.09g
Cholesterol	0mg
Fibre	0.75g

1 Preheat the oven to 200°C/400°F/Gas 6. Bring to boil the apple juice, couscous, sultanas and spice in a pan, stirring. Lower heat, cover and simmer.

COOK'S TIP
Couscous is a pre-cooked wheat that is widely available in supermarkets and health food shops.

2 Spoon half the couscous mixture into a 1.2 litre/2 pint/5 cup ovenproof dish. Peel, core and slice the apples and arrange half the slices over the couscous. Top with the remaining couscous.

3 Arrange the remaining apple slices over the top and sprinkle with demerara sugar. Bake for 25–30 minutes or until golden brown. Serve while still hot, with low-fat yogurt.

BAKED FRUIT COMPOTE

—

**This marvellous medley of dried fruit looks good, tastes even better
and is quick and easy to make.**

INGREDIENTS
115g/4oz/²/3 cup ready-to-eat dried figs
*115g/4oz/¹/2 cup ready-to-eat
dried apricots*
*50g/2oz/¹/2 cup ready-to-eat dried
apple rings*
50g/2oz/¹/4 cup ready-to-eat prunes
50g/2oz/¹/2 cup ready-to-eat dried pears
50g/2oz/¹/2 cup ready-to-eat dried peaches
*300ml/¹/2 pint/1¹/4 cups unsweetened
apple juice*
*300ml/¹/2 pint/1¹/4 cups unsweetened
orange juice*
6 cloves
1 cinnamon stick
a few toasted flaked almonds, to decorate

SERVES 6

1 Preheat the oven to 180°C/350°F/Gas 4.
Place the figs, apricots, apple rings,
prunes, pears and peaches in a shallow
ovenproof dish and stir to mix.

NUTRITIONAL NOTES
Per portion:

Energy	174Kcals/744kJ
Fat, total	0.8g
Saturated fat	0.05g
Cholesterol	0mg
Fibre	5.16g

2 Mix together the unsweetened apple
and orange juices and pour evenly over
the fruit. Add the cloves and cinnamon
stick and stir gently to mix. Make sure
that all the fruit has been thoroughly
coated with the apple and orange juices.

3 Bake for about 30 minutes until the
fruit mixture is hot, stirring once or twice
during cooking. Set aside and leave to
soak for 20 minutes, then remove and
discard the cloves and cinnamon stick.

4 Spoon into serving bowls and serve
warm or cold, decorated with toasted
flaked almonds.

COOK'S TIP
Use other mixtures of unsweetened
fruit juices, such as pineapple and
orange or grape and apple.

KUMQUAT COMPOTE

Warm, spicy and full of sun-ripened ingredients – this is the perfect winter dessert
to remind you of long summer days.

2 Pare the orange rind and add to the pan. Peel and grate the ginger and add to the pan. Crush the cardamom pods and add the seeds to the mixture, with the cloves.

3 Reduce the heat, cover the pan and leave to simmer gently for about 30 minutes, or until the fruit is tender, stirring occasionally.

4 Add the squeezed orange juice to the compote. Sweeten with the honey, sprinkle with the almonds and serve warm.

INGREDIENTS
200g/7oz/2 cups kumquats
200g/7oz/scant 1 cup dried apricots
30ml/2 tbsp sultanas
400ml/14fl oz/1²⁄₃ cups water
1 orange
2.5cm/1in piece of fresh root ginger
4 cardamom pods
4 cloves
30ml/2 tbsp clear honey
15ml/1 tbsp flaked almonds, toasted

SERVES 4

1 Wash the kumquats, and, if they are large, cut them in half. Place them in a pan with the apricots, sultanas and water. Bring to the boil.

NUTRITIONAL NOTES
Per portion:

Energy	198Kcals/833kJ
Fat, total	2.9g
Saturated fat	0.25g
Cholesterol	0mg
Fibre	6.9g

RUSSIAN BLACKCURRANT PUDDING

This fruit pudding from Russia, called Kissel, is traditionally made from the thickened juice of stewed red or blackcurrants. This recipe uses the whole fruit with added blackberry liqueur.

INGREDIENTS
225g/8oz/2 cups red or blackcurrants or
a mixture of both
225g/8oz/2 cups raspberries
150ml/¼ pint/⅔ cup water
50g/2oz/¼ cup caster sugar
25ml/1½ tbsp arrowroot
15ml/1 tbsp crème de mûre
low-fat Greek yogurt, to serve (optional)

SERVES 4

1 Place the currants and raspberries, water and sugar in a pan. Cover the pan and cook over a low heat for 12–15 minutes, until the fruit is soft.

2 Blend the arrowroot to a paste with a little water in a small bowl and stir into the hot fruit mixture. Bring the fruit mixture back to the boil, stirring all the time until thickened and smooth.

3 Remove the pan from the heat and leave the fruit compote to cool slightly, then gently stir in the crème de mûre.

4 Pour the compote into four glass serving bowls and leave until cold, then chill until required. Serve solo or with spoonfuls of low-fat Greek yogurt.

NUTRITIONAL NOTES
Per portion:

Energy	105Kcals/443kJ
Fat, total	0.2g
Saturated fat	0g
Cholesterol	0mg
Fibre	3.3g

COOK'S TIP
Crème de mûre is a blackberry liqueur available from large supermarkets – you could use crème de cassis instead, if you prefer.

CORNFLAKE-TOPPED PEACH BAKE

With just a few storecupboard ingredients, this golden, crisp-crusted, family
pudding can be rustled up in next to no time.

INGREDIENTS
415g/14¹/2 oz can peach slices in juice
30ml/2 tbsp sultanas
1 cinnamon stick
strip of pared orange rind
30ml/2 tbsp low-fat spread
50g/2oz/1¹/2 cups cornflakes
10ml/2 tsp sesame seeds

SERVES 4

1 Preheat the oven to 200°C/400°F/Gas 6.
Drain the peaches, reserving the juice in
a small saucepan. Arrange the peach
slices in a shallow ovenproof dish.

2 Add the sultanas, cinnamon stick and
orange rind to the juice and bring to the
boil. Lower the heat and simmer, for
3–4 minutes, to reduce the liquid by half.
Remove the cinnamon stick and rind and
spoon the syrup over the peaches.

3 Melt the low-fat spread in a small pan,
stir in the cornflakes and sesame seeds.

4 Spread the cornflake mixture over the
fruit. Bake for 15–20 minutes, or until the
topping is crisp and golden. Serve hot.

NUTRITIONAL NOTES
Per portion:

Energy	150Kcals/633kJ
Fat, total	4.6g
Saturated fat	1g
Cholesterol	0.5mg
Fibre	1.3g

RHUBARB SPIRAL COBBLER

The tangy taste of rhubarb combines perfectly with the ginger spice
in this unusual Swiss roll.

3 Roll out the dough on a floured surface
to a 25cm/10in square. Mix the orange
rind, demerara sugar and ginger, then
sprinkle this over the dough.

4 Roll up quite tightly, then cut into
about 10 slices using a sharp knife.
Arrange the slices over the rhubarb.

5 Bake for 20–25 minutes, or until the
spirals are well risen and golden brown.
Serve warm.

INGREDIENTS
675g/1½ lb rhubarb, sliced
45ml/3 tbsp unsweetened orange juice
75g/3oz/6 tbsp caster sugar
200g/7oz/1¾ cups self-raising flour
*about 250ml/8fl oz/1 cup low-fat natural
yogurt*
grated rind of 1 orange
30ml/2 tbsp demerara sugar
5ml/1 tsp ground ginger

SERVES 4

NUTRITIONAL NOTES
Per portion:

Energy	320Kcals/1343kJ
Fat, total	1.2g
Saturated fat	0.34g
Cholesterol	2mg
Fibre	3.92g

1 Preheat the oven to 200°C/400°F/
Gas 6. Mix the rhubarb, orange juice and
50g/2oz/4 tbsp of the caster sugar in a
pan. Cover and cook over a low heat for
10 minutes or until tender. Tip into an
ovenproof dish.

2 To make the topping, mix the flour and
remaining caster sugar in a bowl, then
stir in enough of the yogurt to bind to a
soft dough.

COOK'S TIP
In the summer you could substitute
halved plums, sliced nectarines or
peaches for the rhubarb, if you prefer.

PLUM, APPLE AND BANANA SCONE PIE

This is one of those simple, satisfying puddings that everyone enjoys. It is delicious hot or cold and can be served on its own or with low-fat natural yogurt.

INGREDIENTS
450g/1lb plums
1 Bramley or other cooking apple
1 large banana
150ml/¼ pint/⅔ cup water
115g/4oz/1 cup wholemeal flour, or half
wholemeal and half plain flour
10ml/2 tsp baking powder
25g/1oz/3 tbsp raisins
about 60ml/4 tbsp soured milk or low-fat
natural yogurt
low-fat natural yogurt, to serve (optional)

SERVES 4

2 Mix the fruit in a saucepan. Pour in the water. Bring to simmering point and cook gently for 15 minutes or until the fruit is completely soft.

5 Transfer the scone dough to a lightly floured surface and divide it into 6–8 portions, then pat them into flattish scones.

1 Preheat the oven to 180°C/350°F/Gas 4. Cut the plums in half and ease out the stones. Peel, core and chop the apple, then slice the banana.

3 Spoon the fruit mixture into a pie dish. Level the surface.

6 Cover the plum and apple mixture with the scones. Bake the pie for 40 minutes until the scone topping is cooked through. Serve the pie hot with natural yogurt, or leave it until cold.

4 Mix the flour, baking powder and raisins in a bowl. Add the soured milk or low-fat natural yogurt and mix to a very soft dough.

NUTRITIONAL NOTES
Per portion:

Energy	195Kcals/831kJ
Fat, total	1g
Saturated fat	0.2g
Cholesterol	0.6mg
Fibre	5.2g

COOK'S TIP
To prevent the banana discolouring before cooking, dip each slice in fresh lemon juice.

GRIDDLE CAKES WITH MULLED PLUMS

—

These wonderfully light little pancakes, with their rich, spicy plum sauce, are designed to be cooked on the barbecue, but can just as easily be cooked on the hob.

INGREDIENTS
500g/1¼ lb red plums
90ml/6 tbsp light muscovado sugar
1 cinnamon stick
2 whole cloves
1 piece star anise
90ml/6 tbsp unsweetened apple juice
low-fat Greek yogurt or fromage frais,
to serve (optional)

FOR THE GRIDDLE CAKES
50g/2oz/½ cup plain flour
10ml/2 tsp baking powder
pinch of salt
50g/2oz/½ cup fine cornmeal
30ml/2 tbsp light muscovado sugar
1 egg, beaten
300ml/½ pint/1¼ cups skimmed milk
15ml/1 tbsp corn oil

SERVES 6

1 Halve, stone and quarter the plums. Place them in a pan, with the sugar, spices and apple juice.

COOK'S TIP
Use spray oil on the griddle if you prefer, and cut the fat content still further.

2 Place on a hot barbecue or hob and bring to the boil. Lower heat, cover and simmer gently for 8–10 minutes, stirring, until the plums are soft. Remove the spices and keep the plums warm.

3 For the griddle cakes, sift the flour, baking powder and salt into a large bowl and stir in the cornmeal and sugar.

4 Make a well in the centre and add the egg; gradually beat in the milk. Beat with a whisk or wooden spoon to form a smooth batter. Beat in 5ml/1 tsp of the oil.

5 Heat a griddle or a heavy frying-pan on a hot barbecue or hob. When it is very hot, brush it with some of the remaining oil and then drop tablespoons of batter on to it. Cook the griddle cakes for about a minute, until bubbles start to appear on the surface and the underside is golden.

6 Turn the cakes over and cook the other side for a further minute, or until golden. Bake the other cakes. Serve hot with the mulled plums. Add a spoonful of low-fat Greek yogurt or fromage frais, if you like.

NUTRITIONAL NOTES
Per portion:

Energy	159Kcals/669kJ
Fat, total	3.3g
Saturated fat	0.58g
Cholesterol	33.1mg
Fibre	1.7g

BARBECUED BANANAS WITH SPICY VANILLA SPREAD

Baked bananas are a must for the barbecue – they're so easy because they bake
in their own skins and need no preparation at all.

2 Meanwhile, split the cardamom pods
and remove the seeds. Place the seeds in
a mortar and crush lightly with a pestle.

3 Split the vanilla pod lengthways and
scrape out the tiny seeds. Mix with the
cardamom seeds, orange rind, brandy,
sugar and spread, to make a thick paste.

4 Slit the skin of each banana, open out
slightly and spoon in a little of the paste.
Serve at once.

INGREDIENTS
4 bananas
6 green cardamom pods
1 vanilla pod
finely grated rind of 1 small orange
30ml/2 tbsp brandy
60ml/4 tbsp light muscovado sugar
45ml/3 tbsp low-fat spread

SERVES 4

1 Place the bananas, in their skins, on
the hot barbecue and leave for 6–8
minutes, turning occasionally, until they
are turning brownish-black.

COOK'S TIP
If making this for children, use orange
juice instead of the brandy or, if the fat
content is no object, drizzle the cooked
bananas with melted chocolate.

NUTRITIONAL NOTES
Per portion:

Energy	215Kcals/900kJ
Fat, total	4.9g
Saturated fat	1.22g
Cholesterol	0.7mg
Fibre	1.1g

HOT SPICED BANANAS

Baking bananas in a rum and fruit syrup makes for a dessert with negligible fat and maximum flavour.

INGREDIENTS
low-fat spread, for greasing
6 ripe bananas
200g/7oz/generous 1 cup light brown sugar
250ml/8fl oz/1 cup unsweetened
pineapple juice
120ml/4fl oz/½ cup dark rum
2 cinnamon sticks
12 whole cloves

SERVES 6

NUTRITIONAL NOTES
Per portion:

Energy	290Kcals/1215kJ
Fat, total	0.3g
Saturated fat	0.11g
Cholesterol	0mg
Fibre	1.1g

3 Mix the sugar and pineapple juice in a saucepan. Heat gently until the sugar has dissolved, stirring occasionally. Add the rum, cinnamon sticks and cloves. Bring to the boil, then remove the pan from heat.

4 Pour the hot pineapple and spice mixture over the bananas in the baking dish. Bake in the oven for approximately 25–30 minutes until the bananas are hot and very tender. Serve while still hot.

1 Preheat the oven to 180°C/350°F/Gas 4. Grease a 23cm/9in baking dish.

2 Peel the bananas and cut them diagonally into 2.5cm/1in pieces. Arrange the banana pieces evenly over the bottom of the prepared baking dish.

RUM AND RAISIN BANANAS

—

Choose almost-ripe bananas with evenly coloured skins, either all yellow or just green at the tips.

INGREDIENTS

40g/1¹/2 oz/¹/4 cup seedless raisins
75ml/5 tbsp dark rum
15ml/1 tbsp low-fat spread
60ml/4 tbsp soft light brown sugar
*4 ripe bananas, peeled and halved
lengthways*
1.5ml/¹/4 tsp grated nutmeg
1.5ml/¹/4 tsp ground cinnamon
15ml/1 tbsp slivered almonds, toasted
*low-fat fromage frais or low-fat vanilla
ice cream, to serve (optional)*

SERVES 4

1 Put the raisins in a bowl and pour over the rum. Leave them to soak for about 30 minutes until plump.

2 Melt the spread in a frying pan, add the sugar and stir until it has completely dissolved. Add the bananas and cook for a few minutes until tender, turning occasionally.

3 Sprinkle the spices over the bananas, then pour over the rum and raisins. Carefully set alight using a long-handled match; stir gently to mix.

4 Scatter over the slivered almonds and serve immediately with low-fat fromage frais or low-fat vanilla ice cream, if you like.

COOK'S TIP

For an accompaniment that won't add too much to the fat content of this dessert, make your own yogurt freeze by churning an extra low-fat yogurt in an ice-cream maker.

NUTRITIONAL NOTES

Per portion:

Energy	263Kcals/1110kJ
Fat, total	4.1g
Saturated fat	0.51g
Cholesterol	0.2mg
Fibre	1.6g

CARIBBEAN BANANAS

**Tender baked bananas in a rich and spicy sauce of ground allspice and ginger –
a dessert for those with a sweet tooth!**

INGREDIENTS

30ml/2 tbsp low-fat spread
8 firm ripe bananas
juice of 1 lime
75g/3oz/¹/2 cup soft dark brown sugar
5ml/1 tsp ground allspice
2.5ml/¹/2 tsp ground ginger
seeds from 6 cardamoms crushed
30ml/2 tbsp rum
pared lime rind, to decorate
low-fat crème fraîche, to serve (optional)

SERVES 4

1 Preheat the oven to 200°C/400°F/Gas 6. Use a little of the spread to grease a shallow baking dish large enough to hold the bananas snugly in a single layer.

2 Peel the bananas and cut them in half lengthways. Arrange the bananas in the dish and pour over the lime juice.

3 Mix the sugar, allspice, ginger and crushed cardamom seeds in a bowl. Scatter the mixture over the bananas. Dot with the remaining low-fat spread. Bake, basting once, for 15 minutes, or until the bananas are soft.

4 Remove the dish from the oven. Warm the rum in a small pan or metal soup ladle, pour it over the bananas and set it alight.

5 As soon as the flames die down, decorate the dessert with the pared lime rind. Serve while still hot and add a dollop of low-fat crème fraîche to each portion, if you like.

VARIATION
For a version that will appeal more to children, use orange juice instead of lime and leave out the rum.

NUTRITIONAL NOTES
Per portion:

Energy	310Kcals/1306kJ
Fat, total	3.2g
Saturated fat	0.87g
Cholesterol	0.4mg
Fibre	2.2g

BARBECUED PINEAPPLE BOATS WITH RUM GLAZE

—

Fresh pineapple is even more full of flavour when barbecued or grilled; this spiced rum glaze
turns it into a very special dessert.

INGREDIENTS
1 medium pineapple, about 600g/1lb 6oz
30ml/2 tbsp dark muscovado sugar
5ml/1 tsp ground ginger
45ml/3 tbsp low-fat spread, melted
30ml/2 tbsp dark rum

SERVES 4

COOK'S TIP
For an easier version, cut off the skin
and then slice the whole pineapple into
thick slices and cook as above.

1 With a large, sharp knife, cut the
pineapple lengthways into four equal
wedges. Cut out and discard the hard centre
core from each wedge. Take care when
handling the pineapple's rough outer skin.

2 Cut between the flesh and skin, to
release the flesh, but leave the skin in
place. Slice the flesh across, into chunks.

3 Push a bamboo skewer lengthways
through each wedge and into the stalk,
to hold the chunks in place.

4 Mix together the sugar, ginger, melted
spread and rum and brush over the
pineapple. Cook the wedges on a hot
barbecue for 3–4 minutes; pour the
remaining glaze over the top and serve.

NUTRITIONAL NOTES
Per portion:

Energy	155Kcals/646kJ
Fat, total	4.9g
Saturated fat	1.14g
Cholesterol	0.7mg
Fibre	1.8g

GRILLED NECTARINES WITH AMARETTO

—

Amaretto, the sweet almond-flavoured liqueur from Italy, adds a touch of luxury
to these low-fat grilled nectarines.

INGREDIENTS
6 ripe nectarines
30ml/2 tbsp clear honey
60ml/4 tbsp Amaretto
half-fat crème fraîche, to serve (optional)

SERVES 4

NUTRITIONAL NOTES
Per portion:

Energy	150Kcals/627kJ
Fat, total	0.2g
Saturated fat	0g
Cholesterol	0mg
Fibre	2.7g

1 Cut the nectarines in half by running a small sharp knife down the side of each fruit from top to bottom, pushing the knife right through to the stone. Gently ease the nectarine apart and remove the stone. Try not to handle the fruit too firmly as nectarines bruise easily.

2 Place the nectarines cut side up in an ovenproof dish and drizzle 2.5ml/½ tsp honey and 5ml/1 tsp Amaretto over each half. Preheat the grill until very hot and then grill the fruit until slightly charred. Serve with a little half-fat crème fraîche, if you like.

NECTARINES WITH MARZIPAN AND YOGURT

—

**A luscious dessert that few can resist; marzipan and nectarines are a
wonderful combination.**

INGREDIENTS
4 firm, ripe nectarines or peaches
75g/3oz marzipan
75ml/5 tbsp low-fat Greek yogurt
3 amaretti biscuits, crushed

SERVES 4

3 Spoon the low-fat Greek yogurt on top.
Sprinkle the crushed amaretti biscuits
over the yogurt.

4 Place the fruits on a hot barbecue or
under a hot grill. Cook for 3–5 minutes,
until the yogurt starts to melt.

NUTRITIONAL NOTES	
Per portion:	
Energy	176Kcals/737kJ
Fat, total	4.3g
Saturated fat	0.98g
Cholesterol	3.2mg
Fibre	2.3g

1 Cut the nectarines or peaches in half,
removing the stones.

2 Cut the marzipan into eight pieces and
press one piece into the stone cavity of
each nectarine half. Preheat the grill,
unless you are cooking on the barbecue.

COOK'S TIP
Either peaches or nectarines can be
used for this recipe. If the stone does
not pull out easily when you halve the
fruit, use a small, sharp knife to cut
around it.

SPICED NECTARINES WITH FROMAGE FRAIS

This easy dessert is good at any time of year – use canned peach halves if fresh nectarines are not available.

2 Arrange the fruit, cut-side upwards, in a wide flameproof dish or on a baking sheet.

3 Stir the sugar into the fromage frais. Using a teaspoon, spoon the mixture into the hollow of each half.

4 Sprinkle the fruit with the ground star anise. Place under a moderately hot grill for 6–8 minutes, or until the fruit is hot and bubbling. Serve warm.

INGREDIENTS

4 ripe nectarines or peaches
15ml/1 tbsp light muscovado sugar
115g/4oz/¹/2 cup low-fat fromage frais
2.5ml/¹/2 tsp ground star anise

SERVES 4

1 With a sharp knife cut the nectarines or peaches in half and remove the stones.

NUTRITIONAL NOTES

Per portion:

Energy	108Kcals/450kJ
Fat, total	3.3g
Saturated fat	2g
Cholesterol	14.4mg
Fibre	1.5g

COOK'S TIP

If you can't get star anise, try ground cloves or ground mixed spice.

BARBECUED ORANGE PARCELS

This is one of the most delicious ways of rounding off a barbecue party. The oranges are delicious on their own, but can be served with low-fat fromage frais, if you like.

INGREDIENTS
30ml/2 tbsp low-fat spread, plus extra, melted, for brushing
4 oranges
30ml/2 tbsp maple syrup
30ml/2 tbsp Cointreau or Grand Marnier liqueur
low-fat fromage frais, to serve (optional)

SERVES 4

1 Cut four double-thickness squares of foil, large enough to wrap the oranges. Melt about 10ml/2 tsp of the low-fat spread and brush it over the centre of each piece of foil.

2 Remove some shreds of orange rind, for the decoration. Blanch them, dry them and set them aside. Peel the oranges, removing all the white pith and peel and catching the juice in a bowl.

3 Slice the oranges crossways into several thick slices. Reassemble them and place each orange on a square of foil.

4 Create a cup shape by tucking the foil up high around the oranges. This will keep them in shape, but leave the foil open at the top.

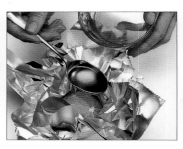

5 Mix together the reserved orange juice, maple syrup and liqueur and spoon the mixture over the oranges.

6 Add a dab of low-fat spread to each parcel and fold over the foil, to seal in the juices. Place the parcels on a hot barbecue for 10–12 minutes, until hot. Serve topped with shreds of orange rind and fromage frais, if you like.

NUTRITIONAL NOTES
Per portion:

Energy	127Kcals/532kJ
Fat, total	3.2g
Saturated fat	0.74g
Cholesterol	0.5mg
Fibre	2.7g

COOK'S TIP
To make the orange shreds for the decoration, slice off several pieces of orange rind, taking care to avoid the bitter white pith, then cut them into thin matchsticks. Add to a small pan of boiling water, for 1 minute, then drain and dry on kitchen paper.

APPLES AND RASPBERRIES IN ROSE SYRUP

Inspiration for this dessert stems from the fact that the apple and the raspberry belong to the rose family. The subtle flavours are shared here in an infusion of rose-scented tea.

INGREDIENTS
5ml/1 tsp rose pouchong tea
900ml/1¹/2 pints/3³/4 cups boiling water
5ml/1 tsp rose-water (optional)
50g/2oz/¹/4 cup granulated sugar
5ml/1 tsp lemon juice
5 dessert apples
175g/6oz/1¹/2 cups fresh raspberries

SERVES 4

1 Warm a large tea pot. Add the rose pouchong tea, then pour on the boiling water, together with the rose-water, if using. Allow to stand and infuse for 4 minutes.

2 Measure the sugar and lemon juice into a stainless steel saucepan. Strain in the tea and stir to dissolve the sugar.

3 Peel and core the apples, then cut into quarters.

4 Poach the apples in the syrup for about 5 minutes.

5 Transfer the apples and syrup to a large metal tray and leave to cool to room temperature.

6 Pour the cooled apples and syrup into a bowl, add the raspberries and mix to combine. Spoon into individual dishes or bowls and serve warm.

NUTRITIONAL NOTES	
Per portion:	
Energy	125Kcals/526kJ
Fat, total	0.4g
Saturated fat	0g
Cholesterol	0mg
Fibre	3.6g

PAPAYA BAKED WITH GINGER

—

Ginger enhances the flavour of papaya in this recipe, which takes no more than
ten minutes to prepare.

INGREDIENTS
2 ripe papayas
2 pieces stem ginger in syrup, drained,
plus 15ml/1 tbsp syrup from the jar
8 dessert biscuits, coarsely crushed
45ml/3 tbsp raisins
shredded, finely pared rind and juice
of 1 lime
15ml/1 tbsp light muscovado sugar
60ml/4 tbsp low-fat Greek yogurt, plus
extra to serve (optional)
15ml/1 tbsp finely chopped unsalted
pistachio nuts

SERVES 4

COOK'S TIP
Don't overcook papaya or the flesh will
become very watery.

1 Preheat the oven to 200°C/400°F/Gas 6.
Cut the papayas in half and scoop out
their seeds. Place the halves in a baking
dish and set aside. Cut the stem ginger
into fine matchsticks.

2 Make the filling. Combine the crushed
biscuits, stem ginger matchsticks and
raisins in a bowl. Make sure they are all
mixed well together.

3 Stir in the lime rind and juice, then add
the sugar and the yogurt. Mix well.

4 Fill the papaya halves and drizzle
with the ginger syrup. Sprinkle with
the pistachios.

5 Bake for about 25 minutes or until
tender. Serve hot, with extra low-fat
Greek yogurt, if you like.

NUTRITIONAL NOTES
Per portion:

Energy	218Kcals/922kJ
Fat, total	4.2g
Saturated fat	1.23g
Cholesterol	6mg
Fibre	3.8g

BAKED PEACHES WITH RASPBERRY SAUCE

**Pretty as a picture – that's the effect when you serve these tasty stuffed peaches
to delighted dinner party guests.**

INGREDIENTS
30ml/2 tbsp low-fat spread
50g/2oz/¹/4 cup granulated sugar
1 egg, beaten
20g/³/4oz/¹/4 cup ground almonds
6 ripe peaches
glossy leaves and plain or frosted
raspberries, to decorate

FOR THE SAUCE
225g/8oz/2 cups raspberries
15ml/1 tbsp icing sugar

SERVES 6

NUTRITIONAL NOTES
Per portion:

Energy	137Kcals/576kJ
Fat, total	4.7g
Saturated fat	0.81g
Cholesterol	32.3mg
Fibre	2.8g

1 Preheat the oven to 180°C/350°F/
Gas 4. Beat the low-fat spread and
sugar together, then beat in the egg
and ground almonds.

2 Cut the peaches in half and remove the
stones. With a spoon, scrape out some of
the flesh from each peach half, slightly
enlarging the hollow left by the stone.
Save the excess peach for the sauce.

3 Stand the peach halves on a baking
sheet, supporting them with crumpled foil
to keep them steady. Fill the hollow in
each peach half with the almond mixture.
Bake for 30 minutes, or until the almond
filling is puffed and golden and the
peaches are very tender.

4 Meanwhile, make the sauce. Combine
the raspberries and icing sugar in a food
processor or blender. Add the reserved
peach flesh. Process until smooth. Press
through a strainer set over a bowl to
remove fibres and seeds.

5 Let the peaches cool slightly. Spoon the
sauce on each plate and arrange two peach
halves on top. Decorate with the leaves
and raspberries and serve immediately.

COOK'S TIP
For a special occasion, stir about
15ml/1 tbsp framboise or peach brandy
into the raspberry sauce.

STUFFED PEACHES WITH ALMOND LIQUEUR

Together amaretti biscuits and amaretto liqueur have an intense almond flavour,
and make a natural partner for peaches.

INGREDIENTS

4 ripe but firm peaches
50g/2oz/¹/₂ cup amaretti biscuits
30ml/2 tbsp low-fat spread
30ml/2 tbsp caster sugar
1 egg yolk
60ml/4 tbsp almond liqueur
low-fat spread, for greasing
250ml/8fl oz/1 cup dry white wine
8 tiny sprigs of fresh basil, to decorate
low-fat ice cream, to serve (optional)

SERVES 4

1 Preheat the oven to 180°C/350°F/Gas 4.
Cut the peaches in half and remove the
stones. With a spoon, scrape out some of
the flesh from each peach half, slightly
enlarging the hollow left by the stone.
Chop this flesh and set it aside.

2 Put the amaretti biscuits in a bowl
and crush them finely with the end of a
rolling pin.

3 Cream the low-fat spread and sugar
together in a separate bowl until smooth.
Stir in the reserved chopped peach flesh,
the egg yolk and half the liqueur with the
amaretti crumbs. Lightly grease a baking
dish that is just large enough to hold the
peach halves in a single layer.

NUTRITIONAL NOTES
Per portion:

Energy	232Kcals/971kJ
Fat, total	5g
Saturated fat	1.37g
Cholesterol	54.7mg
Fibre	1.9g

4 Stand the peaches in the dish and
spoon the stuffing into them. Mix the
remaining liqueur with the wine, pour
over the peaches and bake for 25 minutes
or until the peaches feel tender. Decorate
with basil and serve at once, with low-fat
ice cream, if you like.

COCONUT DUMPLINGS WITH APRICOT SAUCE

—

These delicate little dumplings are very simple to make and cook in minutes. The sharp flavour of the sauce offsets the creamy dumplings beautifully.

INGREDIENTS

75g/3oz/6 tbsp low-fat cottage cheese
1 egg white
15ml/1 tbsp low-fat spread
15ml/1 tbsp light muscovado sugar
30ml/2 tbsp self-raising wholemeal flour
finely grated rind of ¹/2 lemon
15ml/1 tbsp desiccated coconut, toasted

FOR THE SAUCE

225g/8oz can apricot halves in natural juice
15ml/1 tbsp lemon juice

SERVES 4

1 Half-fill a steamer with boiling water and put it on to boil. If you do not own a steamer, place a heatproof plate over a pan of boiling water.

2 Beat together the cottage cheese, egg white and low-fat spread until they are evenly mixed.

3 Stir in the sugar, flour, lemon rind and coconut, mixing everything evenly to a fairly firm dough.

4 Place 8–12 spoonfuls of the mixture in the steamer or on the plate, leaving a space between them.

5 Cover the steamer or pan tightly with a lid or a plate and steam for about 10 minutes, until the dumplings have risen and are firm to the touch.

6 Meanwhile make the sauce. Purée the can of apricots and stir in the lemon juice. Pour into a small pan and heat until boiling, then serve with the dumplings. Sprinkle with extra coconut to serve, if you like and can afford the extra fat.

NUTRITIONAL NOTES
Per portion:

Energy	112Kcals/470kJ
Fat, total	4.3g
Saturated fat	2.56g
Cholesterol	1.2mg
Fibre	1.7g

COOK'S TIP
The mixture should be quite stiff; if it is not stiff enough to hold its shape, stir in a little more flour.

PINEAPPLE FLAMBÉ

—

Flambéing means adding alcohol and then burning it off so the flavour is not too overpowering. This dessert is just as good, however, without the brandy or vodka.

INGREDIENTS

1 large, ripe pineapple, about 600g/1lb 6oz
30ml/2 tbsp low-fat spread
40g/1½ oz/¼ cup soft light brown sugar
60ml/4 tbsp fresh orange juice
30ml/2 tbsp brandy or vodka
15g/½ oz/1 tbsp slivered almonds, toasted

SERVES 4

3 Melt the spread in a frying pan, with the sugar. Add the orange juice. Stir until hot, then add as many pineapple slices as the pan will hold and cook for 1–2 minutes, turning once. As each pineapple slice browns, remove it to a plate.

4 Return all the pineapple slices to the pan, heat briefly, then pour over the brandy or vodka and light with a long-handled match. Let the flames die down, then sprinkle with the almonds. Serve at once.

NUTRITIONAL NOTES
Per portion:

Energy	171Kcals/711kJ
Fat, total	5g
Saturated fat	0.62g
Cholesterol	0.4mg
Fibre	2.1g

1 Cut away the top and base of the pineapple. Then cut down the sides, removing all the dark "eyes".

2 Cut the pineapple into thin slices. Using an apple corer, remove the hard, central core from each slice.

VARIATION
Try this with nectarines, peaches or cherries. Omit the almonds if you want to reduce the fat content a little.

WARM PEARS IN CIDER

There's no fat at all in this delectable dessert. Serve the pears with low-fat Greek yogurt or fromage frais if you must, but they are very good on their own.

INGREDIENTS
1 lemon
50g/2oz/1/4 cup caster sugar
a little grated nutmeg
250ml/8fl oz/1 cup sweet cider
4 firm, ripe pears

SERVES 4

NUTRITIONAL NOTES
Per portion:

Energy	11Kcals/46kJ
Fat, total	0g
Saturated fat	0g
Cholesterol	0mg
Fibre	3.3g

1 Using a potato peeler remove the rind from the lemon in thin strips, leaving any white pith behind.

2 Squeeze the juice from the lemon and pour it into a saucepan. Add the lemon rind, sugar, grated nutmeg and cider and heat gently until the sugar has completely dissolved.

3 Peel the pears, leaving the stalks on if possible, and add them to the pan of cider. Poach the pears for 10–15 minutes until almost tender, turning them frequently.

4 Transfer the pears to individual serving dishes using a slotted spoon. Simmer the liquid over a high heat until it reduces slightly and becomes syrupy. Pour the warm syrup over the pears. Serve at once.

COOK'S TIP
To get pears of just the right firmness, you may have to buy them slightly under-ripe and then wait a day or more. Soft pears are no good at all for this dish.

FANNED POACHED PEARS IN PORT SYRUP

The perfect choice for autumn entertaining, this simple dessert has a beautiful rich colour and fantastic flavour thanks to the tastes of port and lemon.

INGREDIENTS
2 ripe, firm pears
pared rind of 1 lemon
175ml/6fl oz/³/4 cup ruby port
50g/2oz/¹/4 cup caster sugar
1 cinnamon stick
60ml/4 tbsp cold water
half-fat crème fraîche, to serve (optional)

TO DECORATE
15ml/1 tbsp sliced hazelnuts, toasted
fresh mint, pear or rose leaves

SERVES 4

1 Peel the pears, cut them in half and remove the cores. Place the lemon rind, port, sugar, cinnamon stick and water in a shallow pan. Bring to the boil over a low heat. Add the pears, lower the heat, cover and poach for 5 minutes. Let the pears cool in the syrup.

2 When the pears are cold, transfer them to a bowl with a slotted spoon. Return the syrup to the heat. Boil rapidly until it has reduced to form a syrup. Remove the cinnamon stick and lemon rind and leave the syrup to cool.

3 To serve, place each pear half in turn on a board, cut side down. Keeping it intact at the stalk end, slice it lengthways, then, using a palette knife, carefully lift it off and place on a dessert plate. Press gently so that the pear fans out. Spoon over the port syrup. Top each portion with a few hazelnuts and decorate with fresh mint, pear or rose leaves. Serve at once, with half-fat crème fraîche, if you like.

NUTRITIONAL NOTES
Per portion:

Energy	173Kcals/725kJ
Fat	2.5g
Saturated fat	0.17g
Cholesterol	0mg
Fibre	1.9g

MULLED PEARS WITH GINGER AND BRANDY

Serve these pears hot or cold, with lightly whipped cream. The flavours improve with keeping, so you can mull the pears several days before you want to serve them.

INGREDIENTS

600ml/1 pint/2¹/2 cups red wine
225g/8oz/1 cup caster sugar
1 cinnamon stick
6 cloves
finely grated rind of 1 orange
10ml/2 tsp grated fresh root ginger
8 even-sized firm pears, with stalks
15ml/1 tbsp brandy
25g/1oz/¹/4 cup almonds or hazelnuts,
toasted, to decorate
low-fat whipped cream, to serve (optional)

SERVES 8

1 Put all the ingredients except the pears, brandy and nuts into a large pan and heat slowly until the sugar has dissolved. Simmer for 5 minutes.

2 Peel the pears, leaving the stalks on. Arrange them upright in the pan. Cover and simmer until tender, approximately 45–50 minutes, depending on size.

3 Gently remove the pears from the syrup with a slotted spoon, being very careful not to dislodge the stalks. Put the cooked pears in a serving bowl or individual bowls, if you prefer.

NUTRITIONAL NOTES
Per portion:

Energy	246Kcals/1038kJ
Fat, total	1.9g
Saturated fat	0.13g
Cholesterol	0mg
Fibre	3.5g

4 Boil the syrup until it thickens and reduces. Cool slightly, add the brandy and strain over the pears. Decorate with toasted nuts. Serve with whipped cream, if you like.

POACHED PEARS IN MAPLE-YOGURT SAUCE

An elegant dessert that is easier to make than it looks – poach the pears in advance, and have
the cooled syrup ready to spoon on to the plates just before you serve.

INGREDIENTS

6 firm dessert pears
15ml/1 tbsp lemon juice
250ml/8fl oz/1 cup sweet white wine
or cider
thinly pared rind of 1 lemon
1 cinnamon stick
30ml/2 tbsp maple syrup
2.5ml/¹/2 tsp arrowroot
150ml/¹/4 pint/²/3 cup low-fat
Greek yogurt

SERVES 6

1 Peel the pears thinly, leaving them
whole and with the stalks. Brush them
with lemon juice, to prevent them from
browning. Use a potato peeler or small
knife to scoop out the core from the base
of each pear.

2 Place the pears in a wide, heavy pan and
pour over the wine or cider, with enough
cold water to almost cover the pears.

3 Add the lemon rind and cinnamon
stick, then bring to the boil. Reduce the
heat, cover and simmer gently for 30–40
minutes, or until tender. Turn the pears
occasionally so that they cook evenly. Lift
out the pears carefully, draining them well.

4 Boil the liquid uncovered to reduce to
about 120ml/4fl oz/¹/2 cup. Strain into a
jug and add the maple syrup. Blend a
little of the liquid with the arrowroot, then
return the mixture to the jug; mix well.
Return to the pan and cook, stirring, until
thick and clear. Cool.

5 Slice each pear about three-quarters
of the way through, leaving the slices
attached at the stem end. Fan each pear
out on a serving plate.

6 Stir 30ml/2 tbsp of the cooled syrup
into the yogurt and spoon it around the
pears. Drizzle with the remaining syrup
and serve immediately.

COOK'S TIP

The cooking time will vary, depending
upon the type and ripeness of the
pears. The pears should be ripe, but
still firm – over-ripe ones will not keep
their shape well.

NUTRITIONAL NOTES
Per portion:

Energy	136Kcals/573kJ
Fat, total	1.4g
Saturated fat	0.79g
Cholesterol	1.8mg
Fibre	3.3g

BLUSHING PEARS

Pears poached in rosé wine and sweet spices absorb
all the subtle flavours and turn a soft pink colour.

INGREDIENTS
6 firm eating pears
300ml/1/2 pint/11/4 cups rosé wine
150ml/1/4 pint/2/3 cup cranberry juice or
clear apple juice
strip of thinly pared orange rind
1 cinnamon stcik
4 whole cloves
1 bay leaf
75ml/5tbsp caster sugar
small bay leaves, to decorate

SERVES 6

1 Thinly peel the pears with a sharp
knife or vegetable peeler, leaving the
stalks attached.

2 Pour the wine and cranberry or apple
juice into a large heavy-based saucepan.
Add the orange rind, cinnamon stick,
cloves, bay leaf and sugar.

3 Heat gently, stirring all the time until
the sugar has dissolved. Add the pears
and stand them upright in the pan. Pour
in enough cold water to barely cover
them. Cover and cook very gently for
20–30 minutes, or until just tender,
turning and basting occasionally.

4 Using a slotted spoon, gently lift the
pears out of the syrup and transfer to a
serving dish.

5 Bring the syrup to the boil and boil
rapidly for 10-15 minutes, or until it has
reduced by half.

6 Strain the syrup and pour over the
pears. Serve hot, decorated with bay
leaves.

NUTRITIONAL NOTES
Per portion:

Energy	148Kcals/620kJ
Fat, total	0.16g
Saturated fat	0g
Cholesterol	0mg
Fibre	1.9g

COOK'S TIP
Check the pears by piercing with a
skewer or sharp knife towards the end
of the poaching time because some
may cook more quickly than others.

CHAR-GRILLED APPLES ON CINNAMON TOASTS

—

**This yummy treat makes a fabulous finale to a summer barbecue,
but it can also be cooked under the grill.**

INGREDIENTS
4 sweet dessert apples
juice of ¹/₂ lemon
4 individual muffins
15ml/1 tbsp low-fat spread, melted
30ml/2 tbsp golden caster sugar
5ml/1 tsp ground cinnamon
low-fat Greek yogurt, to serve (optional)

SERVES 4

1 Core the apples and cut them
horizontally in three or four thick slices.
Sprinkle with lemon juice.

VARIATION
Other fruit in season could be used for
this recipe. Try pears, peaches or
pineapple for variety. Nutmeg or mixed
spice could also replace the cinnamon.

NUTRITIONAL NOTES
Per portion:

Energy	241Kcals/1016kJ
Fat, total	4.9g
Saturated fat	1.63g
Cholesterol	0.2mg
Fibre	3.0g

2 Cut the muffins into thick slices. Brush
sparingly with melted low-fat spread on
both sides.

3 Mix together the sugar and ground
cinnamon. Preheat the grill if not using
the barbecue.

4 Place the apple and muffin slices on
the hot barbecue or under the grill and
cook them for 3–4 minutes, turning once,
until they are beginning to turn golden
brown.

5 Sprinkle half the cinnamon sugar over
the apple slices and toasts and cook for
1 minute more, until they are a rich
golden brown.

6 To serve, arrange the apple slices over
the toasts and sprinkle them with the
remaining cinnamon sugar. Serve hot,
with low-fat Greek yogurt, if you like.

COOK'S TIP
To keep the quantity of fat within
acceptable levels, make this simple,
scrumptious dessert with muffins, but
for a rare splurge, use brioche or a
similar sweet bread.

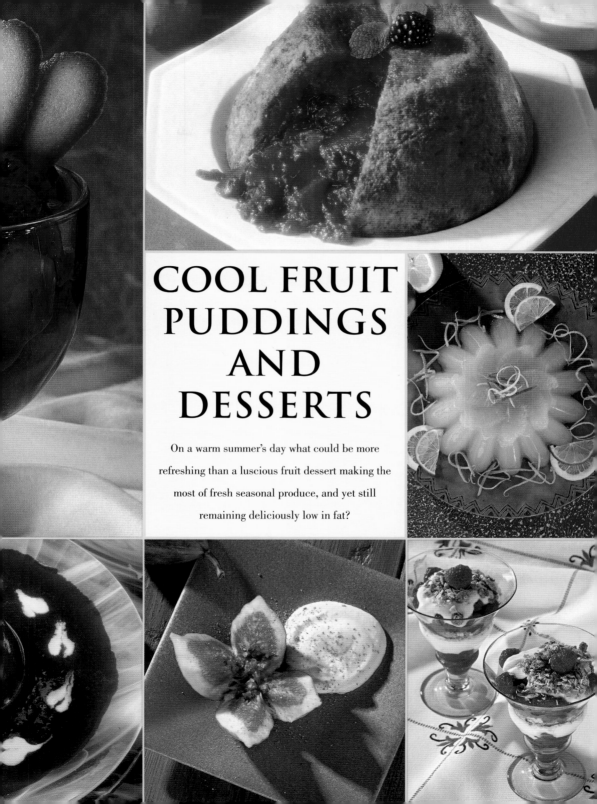

COOL FRUIT PUDDINGS AND DESSERTS

On a warm summer's day what could be more refreshing than a luscious fruit dessert making the most of fresh seasonal produce, and yet still remaining deliciously low in fat?

RICH BLACKCURRANT COULIS

**There can be few more impressive desserts than this –
port wine jelly with swirled cream hearts.**

INGREDIENTS
6 sheets of leaf gelatine
475ml/16fl oz/2 cups water
450g/1lb blackcurrants
225g/8oz/1 cup caster sugar
150ml/¼ pint/⅔ cup ruby port
30ml/2 tbsp crème de cassis
120ml/4fl oz/½ cup single cream,
to decorate

SERVES 8

1 In a small bowl, soak the gelatine in
75ml/5 tbsp of the water until soft. Place
the blackcurrants, sugar and 300ml/
½ pint/1¼ cups of the remaining water
in a large saucepan. Bring to the boil,
lower the heat and simmer for 20 minutes.

2 Strain, reserving the cooking liquid in a
large jug. Put half the blackcurrants in a
bowl and pour over 60ml/4 tbsp of the
reserved cooking liquid. (Freeze the
remaining blackcurrants for another day.)
Set the bowl and jug aside.

3 Squeeze the water out of the gelatine
and place in a small saucepan with the
port, cassis and remaining water. Heat
gently to dissolve the gelatine but do not
allow the mixture to boil. Stir the gelatine
mixture into the jug of blackcurrant
liquid until well mixed.

4 Run 6–8 jelly moulds under cold water,
drain and place in a roasting tin. Fill with
the port mixture. Chill for at least 6 hours
until set. Tip the bowl of blackcurrants
into a food processor, purée until smooth,
then pass through a fine sieve. Taste the
coulis and adjust the sweetness.

5 Run a fine knife around each jelly.
Dip each mould in hot water for 5–10
seconds, then turn the jelly out on to your
hand. Place on a serving plate and spoon
the coulis around the jelly.

6 To decorate, drop a little cream at
intervals on to the coulis. Draw a cocktail
stick through the cream dots, dragging
each in turn into a heart shape. Serve the
desserts immediately.

NUTRITIONAL NOTES
Per portion:

Energy	276Kcals/1163kJ
Fat, total	3.8g
Saturated fat	2.4g
Cholesterol	11mg
Fibre	2.7g

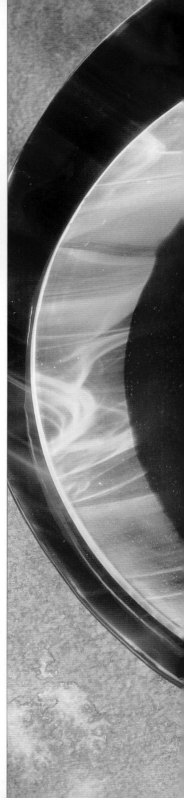

STRAWBERRIES IN SPICED GRAPE JELLY

The spicy cinnamon combines with the sun-ripened strawberries to make a delectable dessert for a summer dinner party.

INGREDIENTS

475ml/16fl oz/2 cups red grape juice
1 cinnamon stick
1 small orange
15ml/1 tbsp powdered gelatine
225g/8oz/2 cups strawberries, chopped,
plus extra to decorate

SERVES 4

1 Pour the grape juice into a pan and add the cinnamon stick. Thinly pare the rind from the orange. Add most of it to the pan but shred some pieces and set them aside for the decoration. Place the pan over a very low heat for 10 minutes, then remove the flavourings from the grape juice.

2 Squeeze the juice from the orange into a bowl and sprinkle over the powdered gelatine. When the mixture is spongy, stir into the grape juice until it has completely dissolved. Allow the jelly to cool in the bowl until just beginning to set.

3 Stir in the strawberries and quickly tip into a 1 litre/1¾ pint/4 cup mould or serving dish. Chill until set.

4 Dip the mould quickly into hot water and invert on to a serving plate. Decorate with strawberries and shreds of orange rind.

NUTRITIONAL NOTES
Per portion:

Energy	85Kcals/355kJ
Fat, total	0.2g
Saturated fat	0g
Cholesterol	0mg
Fibre	1.04g

CHILLED ORANGES IN SYRUP

—

This popular classic is light and simple to make, refreshing and delicious.
A perfect dish to serve after a heavy main course.

2 Cut the orange peel into fine strips and boil in water several times to remove the bitterness. Drain on kitchen paper.

3 Place the water, sugar and lemon juice in a saucepan. Bring to the boil, add the pared orange rind and simmer until the syrup thickens. Add the orange-flower or rose-water, stir and leave to cool.

INGREDIENTS
4 oranges
600ml/1 pint/2¹/2 cups water
350g/12oz/1¹/2 cups granulated sugar
30ml/2 tbsp lemon juice
30ml/2 tbsp orange-flower water or rose-water
40g/1¹/2 oz/¹/3 cup unsalted pistachio nuts, shelled and chopped

SERVES 4

1 Peel the oranges with a potato peeler, avoiding the pith.

NUTRITIONAL NOTES
Per portion:

Energy	467Kcals/1980kJ
Fat, total	4.9g
Saturated fat	0.59g
Cholesterol	0mg
Fibre	3.1g

COOK'S TIP
Almonds could be substituted for the pistachio nuts, if you like, but don't be tempted to increase the quantity or you'll raise the level of fat.

4 Peel away the orange pith and slice. Arrange in a serving dish and pour over the syrup. Chill for 1–2 hours. Sprinkle the pistachio nuts over before serving.

GRAPES IN GRAPE-YOGURT JELLY

—

This light, refreshing combination makes a great special-occasion dessert,
but takes very little time to make.

INGREDIENTS

200g/7oz/1³/4 cups white seedless grapes
450ml/³/4 pint/scant 2 cups unsweetened
white grape juice
15ml/1 tbsp powdered gelatine
120ml/4fl oz/¹/2 cup low-fat
natural yogurt

SERVES 4

1 Set aside four tiny bunches of grapes
for decoration. Pull the rest off their
stalks and cut them in half.

2 Divide the grapes among four stemmed
glasses and tilt the glasses on one side,
propping them firmly in a bowl of ice.

3 Place the grape juice in a pan and heat
it until almost boiling. Remove it from the
heat and sprinkle the gelatine over the
surface, stirring to dissolve the gelatine.

4 Pour half the grape juice over the
grapes and leave to set.

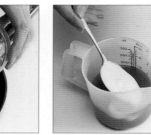

5 Cool the remaining grape juice until
on the verge of setting, then stir in the
low-fat natural yogurt.

6 Stand the set glasses upright and pour
in the yogurt mixture. Chill to set, then
decorate the rim of each glass with
grapes, and serve.

NUTRITIONAL NOTES

Per portion:

Energy	113Kcals/480kJ
Fat, total	0.4g
Saturated fat	0.16g
Cholesterol	1.3mg
Fibre	0g

COOK'S TIP

For an easier version, stand the glasses
upright rather than at an angle – then
they can be put in the fridge to set
rather than packed with ice.

FRESH CITRUS JELLY

**Fresh fruit jellies really are worth the effort – they're packed with fresh flavour,
natural colour and vitamins – and they make a lovely fat-free dessert.**

INGREDIENTS

3 medium oranges
1 lemon
1 lime
300ml/¹/2 pint/1¹/4 cups water
75g/3oz/6 tbsp golden caster sugar
15ml/1 tbsp powdered gelatine
extra slices of citrus fruit,
to decorate

SERVES 4

1 With a sharp knife, cut all the peel and
white pith from one orange and carefully
remove the segments. Arrange the
segments in the base of a 900ml/1¹/2 pint/
3³/4 cup mould or dish. Chill.

2 Remove some shreds of citrus rind with
a zester and reserve them for decoration.
Grate the remaining rind from the lemon
and lime and one orange. Place all the
grated rind in a medium-sized pan, with
the water and sugar.

3 Heat gently, without boiling, until the
sugar has dissolved. Remove from the
heat. Squeeze the juice from all the rest
of the fruit and stir it into the pan.

4 Strain the hot liquid into a measuring
jug to remove the rind. You should have
about 600ml/1 pint/2¹/2 cups of liquid;
if necessary, make up the amount with
hot water. Sprinkle the gelatine over the
liquid and stir until it has dissolved
completely.

5 Pour a little of the jelly over the orange
segments and chill until set. Leave the
remaining jelly at room temperature to
cool, but do not allow it to set.

6 Pour the remaining cooled jelly into the
dish and chill until set. To serve, turn out
the jelly and decorate it with the reserved
citrus rind shreds and extra slices of
citrus fruit.

COOK'S TIP

To speed up the setting of the fruit
segments in jelly, stand the dish in a
bowl of ice. Or, if you're short of time,
simply stir the segments into the liquid
jelly, pour into a serving dish and set it
all together.

NUTRITIONAL NOTES

Per portion:

Energy	137Kcals/580kJ
Fat, total	0.2g
Saturated fat	0g
Cholesterol	0mg
Fibre	2.1g

ORANGE-BLOSSOM JELLY

A fresh orange jelly makes a delightful dessert; the natural fruit flavour
combined with the smooth jelly has a wonderful cleansing quality.

INGREDIENTS
65g/2¹/2 oz/5 tbsp caster sugar
150ml/¹/4 pint/²/3 cup water
25g/1oz powdered gelatine
600ml/1 pint/2¹/2 cups fresh orange juice
30ml/2 tbsp orange-flower water

SERVES 4

3 Gently melt the gelatine over a
saucepan of simmering water until it
becomes clear and transparent. Leave
to cool. When the gelatine is cold, mix
it with the orange juice and orange-
flower water.

1 Place the caster sugar and water in
a small saucepan and heat gently to
dissolve the sugar. Pour into a heatproof
bowl and leave to cool.

4 Wet a jelly mould and pour in the jelly.
Chill in the fridge for at least 2 hours, or
until set. Turn out to serve. If the jelly is
difficult to remove, place the mould in
warm water for a few seconds and the
jelly should come out easily.

2 Sprinkle the gelatine over the surface of
the syrup. Leave to stand until the
gelatine has absorbed all the liquid.

COOK'S TIP
If you are entertaining, make this jelly
extra-special by substituting Grand
Marnier for the orange-flower water.

NUTRITIONAL NOTES
Per portion:

Energy	135Kcals/573kJ
Fat, total	0g
Saturated fat	0g
Cholesterol	0mg
Fibre	0.2g

CLEMENTINE JELLY

Jelly isn't only for children; this adult version has a clear fruity taste and can be made extra special by adding a little white rum or Cointreau.

2 Pour half the juice mixture into a pan. Sprinkle the gelatine on top, leave for 5 minutes, then heat gently until the gelatine has dissolved. Stir in the sugar, then the remaining juice; set aside.

3 Pare the rind very thinly from the remaining fruit and set it aside. Using a sharp knife, cut between the membrane and fruit to separate the citrus segments. Discard the membrane and pith.

4 Place half the segments in four dessert glasses and cover with some of the liquid fruit jelly. Place in the fridge to set.

5 Arrange the remaining segments on top. Carefully pour over the remaining liquid jelly and chill until set. Cut the pared clementine rind into shreds. Serve the jellies topped with a spoonful of crème fraîche scattered with clementine rind shreds.

INGREDIENTS
12 clementines
clear unsweetened white grape juice
(see method for amount)
15ml/1 tbsp powdered gelatine
30ml/2 tbsp caster sugar
60ml/4 tbsp half-fat crème fraîche,
for topping

SERVES 4

VARIATION
Use ruby grapefruit instead of clementines, if you prefer. Squeeze the juice from half and segment the rest.

1 Squeeze the juice from eight of the clementines and pour it into a jug. Make up to 600ml/1 pint/2½ cups with the grape juice, then strain the juice mixture through a fine sieve.

NUTRITIONAL NOTES
Per portion:

Energy	142Kcals/600kJ
Fat, total	2.5g
Saturated fat	1.4g
Cholesterol	15.8mg
Fibre	1.5g

MEXICAN LEMONY RICE PUDDING

Rice pudding is popular the world over and is always different. This Mexican version is light and attractive and very easy to make.

INGREDIENTS

75g/3oz/¹/2 cup raisins
90g/3¹/2 oz/¹/2 cup short-grain (pudding) rice
2.5cm/1in strip of pared lime or lemon rind
250ml/8fl oz/1 cup water
475ml/16fl oz/2 cups skimmed milk
225g/8oz/1 cup granulated sugar
1.5ml/¹/4 tsp salt
2.5cm/1in cinnamon stick
1 egg yolk, well beaten
15ml/1 tbsp low-fat spread
10ml/2 tsp toasted flaked almonds to decorate
orange segments to serve

SERVES 4

3 Discard the cinnamon stick. Drain the raisins well. Add the raisins, egg yolk and low-fat spread, stirring constantly until the spread has been absorbed and the pudding is rich and creamy.

4 Cook the pudding for a few minutes longer. Tip the rice into a serving dish and allow to cool. Decorate with the toasted flaked almonds and serve with the orange segments.

NUTRITIONAL NOTES
Per portion:

Energy	450Kcals/1903kJ
Fat, total	4.9g
Saturated fat	0.88g
Cholesterol	53mg
Fibre	1.4g

1 Put the raisins into a small bowl. Cover with warm water and set aside to soak. Put the rice into a saucepan together with the pared lime or lemon rind and water. Bring slowly to the boil, then lower the heat. Cover the pan and simmer gently for about 20 minutes or until all the water has been absorbed.

2 Remove the rind from the rice and discard it. Add the milk, sugar, salt and cinnamon stick. Cook, stirring, over a very low heat until all the milk has been absorbed. Do not cover the pan.

FRAGRANT RICE WITH DATES

The rice puddings that are popular all over Morocco are served liberally sprinkled with either nuts and honey or wrapped in pastry. This is a low-fat version.

INGREDIENTS

75g/3oz/1/2 cup short-grain (pudding) rice
about 900ml/1 1/2 pints/3 3/4 cups
skimmed milk
30ml/2 tbsp ground rice
50g/2oz/1/4 cup caster sugar
15g/1/2 oz/2 tbsp ground almonds
5ml/1 tsp vanilla essence
2.5ml/1/2 tsp almond essence
a little orange-flower water (optional)
30ml/2 tbsp chopped dates
30ml/2 tbsp unsalted, pistachio nuts,
finely chopped

SERVES 4

1 Place the rice in a saucepan with 750ml/1 1/4 pints/3 cups of the milk and gradually heat until simmering. Cook, uncovered, over a very low heat for 30–40 minutes, until the rice is completely tender, stirring frequently.

2 Blend the ground rice with the remaining milk and add to the pan, stirring. Slowly bring back to the boil and cook for 1 minute.

3 Stir in the sugar, ground almonds, vanilla and almond essences and orange-flower water, if using. Cook until the pudding is thick and creamy.

4 Pour into serving bowls and sprinkle with the chopped dates and pistachios. Allow to cool before serving.

NUTRITIONAL NOTES
Per portion:

Energy	270Kcals/1135kJ
Fat, total	4.8g
Saturated fat	0.55g
Cholesterol	4.5mg
Fibre	0.4g

RICE PUDDING WITH MIXED BERRY SAUCE

**A compote of red berries contrasts beautifully with creamy rice pudding
for a richly flavoured cool dessert.**

INGREDIENTS

low-fat spread, for greasing
*400g/14oz/2 cups short-grain
(pudding) rice*
*325ml/11fl oz/scant 1½ cups
skimmed milk*
pinch salt
115g/4oz/⅔ cup soft light brown sugar
5ml/1 tsp pure vanilla essence
2 eggs, beaten
grated rind of 1 lemon
5ml/1 tsp lemon juice
30ml/2 tbsp low-fat spread
strawberry leaves, to decorate

FOR THE SAUCE

*225g/8oz/2 cups strawberries, hulled
and quartered*
225g/8oz/2 cups raspberries
115g/4oz/½ cup granulated sugar
grated rind of 1 lemon

SERVES 6

1 Preheat the oven to 160°C/325°F/Gas 3.
Grease a deep 2 litre/3½ pint/8 cup
baking dish. Add the rice to boiling water
and boil for 5 minutes. Drain. Transfer
the rice to the prepared baking dish.

2 Combine the milk, salt, brown sugar,
vanilla essence, eggs, and lemon rind and
juice. Pour over the rice and stir.

3 Dot the surface of the rice mixture with
the spread. Bake for about 50 minutes
until the rice is cooked and creamy.

4 Meanwhile, make the sauce. Mix the
berries and sugar in a small saucepan.
Stir over low heat until the sugar dissolves
completely and the fruit is becoming pulpy.

5 Transfer to a bowl and stir in the lemon
rind. Cool, then chill until required.

6 Remove the rice pudding from the
oven. Leave to cool. Serve with the berry
sauce. Decorate with strawberry leaves.

NUTRITIONAL NOTES
Per portion:

Energy	474Kcals/1991kJ
Fat, total	4.9g
Saturated fat	0.95g
Cholesterol	65.5mg
Fibre	1.4g

FRESH FRUIT WITH CARAMEL RICE

Creamy rice pudding with a crisp caramel crust sounds wickedly indulgent, but is relatively low in fat, especially if you serve fairly small portions, with fresh fruit.

INGREDIENTS

50g/2oz/generous ¼ cup short-grain (pudding) rice
low-fat spread, for greasing
75ml/5 tbsp demerara sugar
pinch of salt
400g/14oz can light evaporated milk made up to 600ml/1 pint/2½ cups with water
2 crisp eating apples
1 small fresh pineapple
10ml/2 tsp lemon juice

SERVES 4

1 Preheat the oven to 150°C/300°F/Gas 2. Wash the rice under cold water. Drain well and put into a lightly greased soufflé dish.

2 Add 30ml/2 tbsp of the sugar to the dish, with the salt. Pour on the diluted evaporated milk and stir gently. Bake for 2 hours, then leave to cool for 30 minutes.

3 Meanwhile, peel, core and cut the apples and pineapple into thin slices, then cut the pineapple into chunks. Toss the fruit in lemon juice, coating thoroughly, and set aside.

4 Preheat the grill and sprinkle the remaining sugar over the rice. Grill for 5 minutes to caramelize the sugar. Leave to stand for 5 minutes to harden the caramel. Serve with the fresh fruit.

NUTRITIONAL NOTES

Per portion:

Energy	309Kcals/1293kJ
Fat, total	4.6g
Saturated fat	2.51g
Cholesterol	34mg
Fibre	2.8g

RICE FRUIT SUNDAE

Cook a rice pudding on top of the stove instead of in the oven for a light creamy texture,
which is particularly good served cold topped with fruits.

INGREDIENTS

50g/2oz/¹/3 cup short-grain
(pudding) rice
600ml/1 pint/2¹/2 cups skimmed milk
5ml/1 tsp pure vanilla essence
2.5ml/¹/2 tsp ground cinnamon
25g/1oz/2 tbsp granulated sugar
200g/7oz/1³/4 cups strawberries,
raspberries or blueberries, to serve

SERVES 4

1 Put the rice, milk, vanilla essence,
cinnamon and sugar into a medium-sized
saucepan. Bring to the boil, stirring
constantly, and then turn down the heat
so that the mixture barely simmers.

2 Cook the rice for 30–40 minutes,
stirring occasionally, until the grains are
soft. Tip into a bowl and allow the rice to
cool, stirring occasionally. When cold,
chill the rice in the fridge.

NUTRITIONAL NOTES
Per portion:

Energy	169Kcals/711kJ
Fat, total	3.3g
Saturated fat	0.1g
Cholesterol	3mg
Fibre	0.9g

3 Just before serving, stir the rice and
spoon into four sundae dishes. Top with
the prepared fruit.

VARIATION
Instead of simple pudding rice try
using a Thai fragrant or jasmine rice
for a delicious natural flavour. For a
firmer texture, an Italian arborio rice
makes a good pudding too. You could
also use other toppings, such as
toasted, chopped hazelnuts or toasted
coconut flakes. Other fruit combinations
could be mango, pineapple and banana
for a tropical taste.

SUMMER PUDDING

Summer pudding is an annual treat, and need not be high in fat if you avoid serving it with lashings of cream.

Ingredients

*1 loaf of white crusty bread,
1–2 days old, sliced
675g/1¹/2 lb/6 cups fresh redcurrants
75g/3oz/6 tbsp granulated sugar
60ml/4 tbsp water
450g/1lb/4 cups mixed berries, plus extra
to decorate
sprig of mint, to decorate
juice of ¹/2 lemon*

Serves 6

Nutritional Notes

Per portion:

Energy	272Kcals/1152kJ
Fat, total	1.6g
Saturated fat	0g
Cholesterol	0mg
Fibre	7.6g

1 Trim the crusts from the bread slices. Cut a round of bread to fit in the bottom of a 1.5 litre/2¹/2 pint/6-cup pudding basin. Line the basin with bread slices, overlapping them slightly. Reserve enough bread slices to cover the top of the basin. Mix the redcurrants with 50g/2oz/¹/4 cup of the sugar and the water in a non-reactive saucepan. Heat gently, crushing the berries lightly to help the juices flow. When the sugar has dissolved, remove from the heat.

2 Tip the redcurrant mixture into a food processor and process until quite smooth. Press through a fine-mesh nylon strainer set in a bowl. Discard the fruit pulp left in the strainer.

3 Put the mixed berries in a bowl with the remaining sugar and the lemon juice. Stir well.

4 One at a time, remove the cut bread pieces from the basin and dip them in the redcurrant purée. Replace to line the basin evenly.

5 Spoon the berries into the lined basin, pressing them down evenly. Top with the reserved cut bread slices, which have been dipped in the redcurrant purée.

6 Cover the basin with clear film. Set a small plate, just big enough to fit inside the rim of the basin, on top of the pudding. Weigh it down with cans of food. Chill in the fridge for 8–24 hours.

7 To turn out, remove the weights, plate and clear film. Run a knife between the basin and the pudding to loosen it. Invert on to a serving plate. Decorate with a sprig of mint and a few berries. Serve in wedges.

AUTUMN PUDDING

Summer pudding is far too good to be reserved for the soft fruit season. Here is an autumn version, with apples, plums and blackberries.

INGREDIENTS

450g/1lb eating apples
450g/1lb plums, halved and stoned
225g/8oz/2 cups blackberries
60ml/4 tbsp apple juice
sugar or honey, to sweeten (optional)
8 slices of wholemeal bread, crusts removed
mint sprig and blackberry, to decorate
half-fat crème fraîche, to serve (optional)

SERVES 6

3 Spoon the fruit into the basin. Pour in just enough juice to moisten. Reserve any remaining juice.

4 Cover the fruit completely with the remaining bread. Fit a plate on top, so that it rests on the bread just below the rim. Stand the basin in a larger bowl to catch any juice. Place a weight on the plate and chill overnight.

5 Turn the pudding out on to a plate and pour the reserved juice over any areas that have not absorbed the juice. Decorate with the mint sprig and blackberry. Serve with crème fraîche, if you like.

1 Quarter the apples, remove the cores and peel, then slice them into a saucepan. Add the plums, blackberries and apple juice. Cover and cook gently for 10–15 minutes until tender. Sweeten, if necessary, with a little sugar or honey, although the fruit should be sweet enough.

2 Line the bottom and sides of a 1.2 litre/ 2 pint/5 cup pudding basin with slices of bread, cut to fit. Press together tightly.

NUTRITIONAL NOTES
Per portion:

Energy	141Kcals/595kJ
Fat, total	1.1g
Saturated fat	0.17g
Cholesterol	0mg
Fibre	5.4g

TWO-TONE YOGURT RING WITH TROPICAL FRUIT

An impressive, light and colourful dessert with a truly tropical flavour,
combining mango, kiwi fruit and physalis together.

INGREDIENTS
175ml/6fl oz/³/4 cup tropical fruit juice
15ml/1 tbsp powdered gelatine
3 egg whites
150ml/¹/4 pint/²/3 cup low-fat
natural yogurt
finely grated rind of 1 lime

FOR THE FILLING
1 mango
2 kiwi fruit
10–12 physalis (Cape gooseberries),
plus extra to decorate
juice of 1 lime

SERVES 6

1 Pour the tropical fruit juice into a small pan and sprinkle the powdered gelatine over the surface. Heat gently until the gelatine has dissolved.

NUTRITIONAL NOTES
Per portion:

Energy	87Kcals/364kJ
Fat, total	0.5g
Saturated fat	0.13g
Cholesterol	1mg
Fibre	2.3g

2 Whisk the egg whites in a grease-free bowl until they hold soft peaks. Continue whisking hard, gradually adding the yogurt and lime rind.

3 Continue whisking hard and pour in the hot gelatine mixture in a steady stream, until evenly mixed.

4 Quickly pour the mixture into a 1.5 litre/2¹/2 pint/6¹/4 cup ring mould. Chill the mould in the fridge until set. The mixture will separate into two layers.

5 Prepare the filling. Halve, stone, peel and dice the mango. Peel and slice the kiwi fruit. Remove the husks from the physalis (Cape gooseberries) and cut them in half. Toss all the fruits together in a bowl and stir in the lime juice.

6 Run a knife around the edge of the ring to loosen the mixture. Dip the tin quickly into hot water, then turn it out on to a serving plate. Spoon all the prepared fruit into the centre of the ring, decorate with the reserved physalis and serve immediately.

VARIATION
Any mixture of fruit works in this recipe, depending on the season. Try using apple juice in the ring mixture and fill it with luscious, red summer fruits.

FRUITED RICE RING

**This unusual rice pudding looks beautiful turned out of a ring mould but if you prefer, stir the
fruit into the rice and serve in individual dishes.**

2 Meanwhile, mix the dried fruit salad
and orange juice in a pan and bring to the
boil. Cover, then simmer very gently for
about 1 hour, until tender and no free
liquid remains.

3 Remove the cinnamon stick from the
rice and stir in the sugar and orange rind,
mixing thoroughly.

4 Tip the fruit into the base of a lightly
oiled 1.5 litre/2½ pint/6¼ cup ring
mould. Spoon the rice over, smoothing
down firmly. Chill.

5 Run a knife around the edge of the
mould and turn out the rice carefully on
to a serving plate.

INGREDIENTS
65g/2½ oz/5 tbsp short-grain
(pudding) rice
900ml/1½ pints/3¾ cups
semi-skimmed milk
1 cinnamon stick
175g/6oz/1½ cups dried fruit salad
350ml/12fl oz/1½ cups orange juice
45ml/3 tbsp caster sugar
finely grated rind of 1 small orange
low-fat oil, for greasing

SERVES 4

1 Mix the rice, milk and cinnamon stick
in a large pan and bring to the boil. Lower
the heat, cover and simmer, stirring
occasionally, for about 1½ hours, until
no free liquid remains.

NUTRITIONAL NOTES
Per portion:

Energy	343Kcals/1440kJ
Fat, total	4.4g
Saturated fat	2.26g
Cholesterol	15.75mg
Fibre	1.07g

DRIED FRUIT FOOL

This light, fluffy dessert can be made with a single dried fruit – try dried peaches,
prunes, apples or apricots.

INGREDIENTS

*300g/11oz/1¼ cups ready-to-eat
dried fruit such as apricots, peaches,
prunes or apples*
300ml/½ pint/1¼ cups fresh orange juice
250ml/8fl oz/1 cup low-fat fromage frais
2 egg whites
fresh mint sprigs, to decorate

SERVES 4

NUTRITIONAL NOTES

Per portion:

Energy	180Kcals/757kJ
Fat, total	0.63g
Saturated fat	0.06g
Cholesterol	0.5mg
Fibre	4.8g

3 Whisk the egg whites in a grease-free
bowl until stiff enough to hold soft peaks,
then slowly fold into the fruit mixture
until it is all combined.

4 Spoon into four stemmed glasses or
one large serving dish. Chill for at least
1 hour. Decorate with the mint sprigs just
before serving.

COOK'S TIP

To make a speedier fool leave out the
egg whites and simply swirl together
the fruit mixture and fromage frais.

1 Put the dried fruit in a saucepan, add
the orange juice and heat gently until
boiling. Lower the heat, cover and simmer
gently for 3 minutes.

2 Cool slightly. Tip into a food processor
or blender and process until smooth. Stir
in the fromage frais.

PASSION FRUIT AND APPLE FOAM

**Passion fruit have an exotic, scented flavour that really lifts this simple apple dessert.
If passion fruit are not available, use two finely chopped kiwi fruit instead.**

INGREDIENTS
450g/1lb cooking apples
90ml/6 tbsp unsweetened apple juice
3 passion fruit
3 egg whites
1 red-skinned eating apple, to decorate
5ml/1 tsp lemon juice

SERVES 4

1 Peel, core and roughly chop the cooking apples. Put them in a pan with the apple juice.

2 Bring the liquid to the boil, then lower the heat and cover the pan. Cook gently, stirring occasionally, until the apple is very tender.

3 Remove from the heat and beat the apple mixture with a wooden spoon until it forms a fairly smooth purée (or purée the apple in a food processor if you prefer).

4 Cut the passion fruit in half and scoop out the flesh. Stir the flesh into the apple purée to mix thoroughly.

5 Place the egg whites in a grease-free bowl and whisk them until they form soft peaks. Fold the egg whites into the apple mixture. Spoon the apple foam into four serving dishes. Leave to cool.

6 Thinly slice the red-skinned apple and brush the slices with lemon juice to prevent them from browning. Arrange the slices on top of the apple foam and serve cold.

COOK'S TIP
It is important to use a good cooking apple, such as a Bramley, for this recipe, because the fluffy texture of a cooking apple breaks down easily to a purée. You can use dessert apples, but will probably have to purée them in a food processor.

NUTRITIONAL NOTES
Per portion:

Energy	80Kcals/338kJ
Fat, total	0.2g
Saturated fat	0g
Cholesterol	0mg
Fibre	2.9g

RASPBERRY AND MINT BAVAROIS

A sophisticated dessert that can be made a day in advance for a special dinner party.

INGREDIENTS
*450g/1lb/4 cups fresh or
thawed frozen raspberries
30ml/2 tbsp icing sugar
30ml/2 tbsp lemon juice
15ml/1 tbsp finely chopped fresh mint
30ml/2 tbsp powdered gelatine
75ml/5 tbsp boiling water
300ml/¹/₂ pint/1¹/₄ cups low-fat custard
250ml/8fl oz/1 cup low-fat Greek yogurt
fresh mint sprigs, to decorate*

SERVES 6

1 Reserve a few raspberries for decoration. Place the remaining raspberries in a food processor. Add the icing sugar and lemon juice and process to a smooth purée.

2 Press the purée through a sieve to remove the raspberry seeds. Pour it into a measuring jug and stir in the mint.

3 Sprinkle 5ml/1 tsp of the gelatine over 30ml/2 tbsp of the boiling water and stir until the gelatine has dissolved. Stir into 150ml/¹/₄ pint/²/₃ cup of the fruit purée.

4 Pour this jelly into a 1 litre/1³/₄ pint/4 cup mould, and chill in the fridge until the jelly is just setting. Tip the tin to swirl the setting jelly around the sides, and leave to chill until the jelly has set completely.

5 Mix the custard and low-fat Greek yogurt in a bowl and stir in the remaining fruit purée. Dissolve the rest of the gelatine in the remaining boiling water and stir it in quickly.

6 Pour the raspberry custard into the mould and chill it until it has set completely. To serve, dip the mould quickly into hot water and then turn it out on a serving plate. Decorate with the reserved raspberries and the mint sprigs.

NUTRITIONAL NOTES
Per portion:

Energy	131Kcals/554kJ
Fat, total	2.4g
Saturated fat	1.36g
Cholesterol	4.1mg
Fibre	1.9g

COOK'S TIP
You can make this dessert using frozen raspberries, which have a good colour and flavour. Allow them to thaw at room temperature, and use any juice in the jelly.

BRAZILIAN COFFEE BANANAS

—

Rich, lavish and sinful-looking, this low-fat dessert takes only about
2 minutes to make!

INGREDIENTS

4 small ripe bananas
15ml/1 tbsp instant coffee granules
or powder
15ml/1 tbsp hot water
30ml/2 tbsp dark muscovado sugar
250ml/8fl oz/1 cup low-fat Greek yogurt
10ml/2 tsp toasted flaked almonds

SERVES 4

NUTRITIONAL NOTES
Per portion:

Energy	175Kcals/736kJ
Fat, total	4.8g
Saturated fat	2.06g
Cholesterol	4.4mg
Fibre	1.1g

1 Peel and slice one banana and peel and mash the remaining three with a fork. Dissolve the coffee in the hot water and stir into the mashed bananas.

VARIATION

For a special occasion, add a dash of dark rum or brandy to the bananas. 15ml/ 1 tbsp of rum or brandy won't affect the amount of fat, but will add 30 calories.

2 Spoon a little of the mashed banana mixture into four serving dishes and sprinkle each with sugar. Top with a spoonful of yogurt, then repeat the layers until all the ingredients are used up.

3 Swirl the last layer of yogurt for a marbled effect. Finish with a few banana slices and flaked almonds. Serve cold. This dish is best eaten within about an hour of making.

RASPBERRY MUESLI LAYER
—

**As well as being a delicious, low-fat dessert, this can be made in advance
and stored in the fridge overnight to be served for a quick, healthy breakfast.**

INGREDIENTS
*225g/8oz/2 cups fresh or frozen and
thawed raspberries*
250ml/8fl oz/1 cup low-fat natural yogurt
75g/3oz/¹/₂ cup Swiss-style muesli

SERVES 4

3 Sprinkle a layer of Swiss-style muesli
over the yogurt.

4 Continue the layers until all the
ingredients have been used. Top each
dessert with a whole raspberry.

1 Reserve four raspberries for decoration,
then spoon a few raspberries into four
stemmed glasses or glass dishes.

2 Top the raspberries in each glass with a
spoonful of yogurt.

NUTRITIONAL NOTES
Per portion:

Energy	114Kcals/481kJ
Fat, total	1.7g
Saturated fat	0.48g
Cholesterol	2.3mg
Fibre	2.6g

CLEMENTINES IN CINNAMON CARAMEL

—

The combination of sweet, yet sharp clementines and caramel sauce with a hint of spice is divine.
Served with low-fat Greek-style yogurt or crème fraîche, this makes a delicious dessert.

INGREDIENTS

8–12 clementines, about 450–500g/
1–1¼ lb
225g/8oz/1 cup granulated sugar
300ml/½ pint/1¼ cups warm water
2 cinnamon sticks
30ml/2 tbsp orange-flavoured liqueur
25g/1oz/¼ cup shelled, unsalted
pistachio nuts

SERVES 4

1 Using a vegetable peeler pare the rind
from two clementines and cut it into fine
strips. Set aside.

2 Peel the clementines, removing all the
pith but keeping each fruit intact. Put the
fruits in a heatproof serving bowl.

3 Gently heat the sugar in a pan until it
dissolves and turns a rich golden brown.
Immediately turn off the heat.

4 Protecting your hand with a dish towel,
carefully pour in the warm water (the
mixture will bubble and splutter). Bring
slowly to the boil, stirring until all the
caramel has dissolved.

5 Add the shredded peel and cinnamon
sticks, then simmer for 5 minutes. Stir in
the orange-flavoured liqueur.

6 Leave the syrup to cool for about
10 minutes, then pour it over the
clementines. Cover the bowl, cool, then
chill for several hours or overnight.

7 Blanch the unsalted pistachio nuts in
boiling water. Drain, cool and remove
outer skins. Decorate the clementines
by scattering the nuts over the top.
Serve at once.

NUTRITIONAL NOTES

Per portion:

Energy	328Kcals/1392kJ
Fat, total	3.5g
Saturated fat	0.42g
Cholesterol	0mg
Fibre	1.4g

YOGURT WITH APRICOTS AND PISTACHIOS

If you allow a yogurt to drain overnight, it becomes thicker and more luscious. Add honeyed apricots and nuts, and you have an exotic yet simple dessert.

INGREDIENTS
250ml/8fl oz/1 cup low-fat Greek yogurt
250ml/8fl oz/1 cup low-fat natural yogurt
175g/6oz/3/4 cup ready-to-eat dried
apricots, snipped
15ml/1 tbsp clear honey
10ml/2 tsp roughly chopped unsalted
pistachio nuts, plus extra for sprinkling
ground cinnamon, for sprinkling

SERVES 4

1 Mix the yogurts and place in a sieve over a bowl. Drain overnight in the fridge.

2 Discard the yogurt whey. Place the apricots in a saucepan, cover with water and simmer to soften. Drain, cool, then tip into a bowl and stir in the honey.

3 Add the yogurt to the apricot mixture, with the nuts. Spoon into sundae dishes, sprinkle over a little cinnamon and nuts and chill. Serve chilled.

NUTRITIONAL NOTES
Per portion:

Energy	164Kcals/689kJ
Fat, total	4.5g
Saturated fat	2g
Cholesterol	5.5mg
Fibre	2.8g

RASPBERRIES AND FRUIT PURÉE

—

Three fruit purées, swirled together, make a
kaleidoscopic garnish for a nest of raspberries.

INGREDIENTS
200g/7oz raspberries
120ml/4fl oz/¹/₂ cup red wine
icing sugar, for dusting

FOR THE DECORATION
1 large mango, peeled and chopped
400g/14oz kiwi fruit, peeled and chopped
200g/7oz raspberries
icing sugar, to taste

SERVES 4–6

3 Spoon each purée on to a serving plate,
separating the kiwi and mango with the
raspberry purée as if creating a four-
wedged pie. Gently tap the plate on the
work surface to settle the purées against
each other.

1 Place the raspberries in a bowl with the
red wine and allow to macerate for about
2 hours.

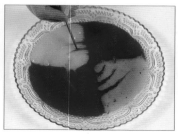

4 Using a skewer, draw a spiral outwards
from the centre of the plate to the rim.
Drain the macerated raspberries, pile
them in the centre, and dust them heavily
with icing sugar.

2 Make the decoration. Purée the mango
in a food processor, adding water if
necessary. Press through a sieve into a
bowl. Purée the kiwi fruit in the same way,
then make a third purée from the remaining
raspberries. Sweeten the purées with
sifted icing sugar, if necessary.

NUTRITIONAL NOTES
Per portion:

Energy	154Kcals/648kJ
Fat, total	0.9g
Saturated fat	0g
Cholesterol	0mg
Fibre	6.7g

CRISMON PEARS

*Poached pears in red wine are among the simplest of sweet treats,
but look spectacular.*

INGREDIENTS
1 bottle of red wine
175g/6oz/³/4 cup granulated sugar
45ml/3 tbsp clear honey
juice of ¹/2 lemon
1 cinnamon stick
1 vanilla pod, split lengthways
5cm/2in piece of pared orange rind
1 whole clove
1 black peppercorn
4 firm, ripe pears
low-fat Greek yogurt, to serve (optional)
mint leaves, to decorate

SERVES 4

1 In a large saucepan combine the wine, sugar, honey, lemon juice, cinnamon, vanilla pod, orange rind, clove and peppercorn. Heat gently, stirring occasionally until the sugar dissolves.

2 Meanwhile, peel the pears, leaving the cores and stems intact. Slice a small piece off the base of each pear so it will stand upright.

3 Gently place the pears in the wine mixture. Simmer uncovered for 20–35 minutes, until the pears are just tender.

4 With a slotted spoon, gently transfer the pears to a bowl. Continue to boil the poaching liquid until reduced by about half. Tip into a jug and leave to cool.

5 Strain the cooled liquid over the pears. Chill for at least 3 hours.

6 Place the pears in serving dishes, spoon over the liquid and decorate with a mint leaf. Serve solo or with low-fat Greek yogurt.

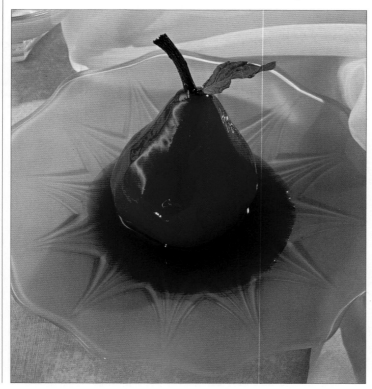

NUTRITIONAL NOTES
Per portion:

Energy	398Kcals/1681kJ
Fat, total	0.2g
Saturated fat	0g
Cholesterol	0mg
Fibre	3.3g

APPLE FOAM WITH BLACKBERRIES

—

This lovely light dish is perfect if you fancy a dessert, but don't want anything
too rich or too filling.

INGREDIENTS
225g/8oz/2 cups blackberries
150ml/¹/4 pint/²/3 cup unsweetened
apple juice
5ml/1 tsp powdered gelatine
15ml/1 tbsp clear honey
2 egg whites

SERVES 4

1 Place the blackberries in a pan with
60ml/4 tbsp of the apple juice and heat
gently until the fruit is soft. Remove from
the heat, cool, then chill.

2 Sprinkle the gelatine over the
remaining apple juice in a small pan and
stir over low heat until dissolved. Stir in
the honey.

3 Whisk the egg whites until they hold
stiff peaks. Continue whisking hard and
pour in the hot gelatine mixture gradually,
until well mixed.

4 Quickly spoon the foam into rough
mounds on individual plates. Chill.
Serve with the blackberries and juice
spooned around.

NUTRITIONAL NOTES
Per portion:

Energy	49Kcals/206kJ
Fat, total	0.2g
Saturated fat	0g
Cholesterol	0mg
Fibre	1.7g

SENSATIONAL STRAWBERRIES

Strawberries release their finest flavour when moistened
with a sauce of raspberries and passion fruit.

INGREDIENTS
*350g/12oz/3 cups raspberries, fresh
or frozen
45ml/3 tbsp caster sugar
1 passion fruit
675g/1¹/₂ lb small strawberries
dessert biscuits, to serve (optional)*

SERVES 4

1 Mix the raspberries and sugar in a
saucepan and heat gently until the
raspberries release their juices. Simmer
for 5 minutes. Leave to cool.

2 Cut the passion fruit in half and scoop
out the seeds and juice into a bowl.

COOK'S TIP
Berry fruits taste best at room
temperature; take them out of the fridge
at least half an hour before serving.

3 Tip the raspberry mixture into a food
processor or blender, add the passion
fruit and blend to a smooth purée.

4 Press the purée through a fine nylon
sieve placed over a bowl, to remove
the seeds.

5 Fold the strawberries into the sauce,
then spoon into four stemmed glasses.
Serve with the dessert biscuits, if you
like, but these will increase the fat
content of the dessert.

NUTRITIONAL NOTES
Per portion:

Energy	115Kcals/484kJ
Fat, total	0.5g
Saturated fat	0g
Cholesterol	0mg
Fibre	4.2g

GREEK FIG AND HONEY PUDDING

—

A quick and easy pudding made from fresh figs topped with yogurt, drizzled with honey and sprinkled with pistachio nuts.

1 Chop the figs and place in the bottom of four stemmed glasses or deep, individual dessert bowls.

2 Stir the Greek yogurt and natural yogurt together. Top each glass or bowl of figs with a quarter of the mixture. Chill until ready to serve.

3 Just before serving drizzle 15ml/1 tbsp honey over each dessert and sprinkle with the pistachio nuts.

INGREDIENTS
4 fresh figs
250ml/8fl oz/1 cup low-fat Greek yogurt
250ml/8fl oz/1 cup low-fat natural yogurt
60ml/4 tbsp clear honey
10ml/2 tsp chopped, unsalted pistachio nuts

SERVES 4

NUTRITIONAL NOTES
Per portion:

Energy	158Kcals/664kJ
Fat, total	4.7g
Saturated fat	2.21g
Cholesterol	6.1mg
Fibre	0.8g

COOK'S TIP
Look out for specialist honeys made from the nectar of flowers like lavender, clover, acacia, heather, rosemary and thyme.
If unsalted pistachios are difficult to find, substitute chopped walnuts or almonds instead.

FIGS WITH RICOTTA CREAM

Fresh, ripe figs are full of natural sweetness. This simple recipe makes the most of their beautiful, intense flavour.

INGREDIENTS
4 ripe, fresh figs
115g/4oz/¹/2 cup ricotta cheese
45ml/3 tbsp half-fat crème fraîche
15ml/1 tbsp clear honey
2.5ml/¹/2 tsp pure vanilla essence
freshly grated nutmeg, to decorate

SERVES 4

COOK'S TIP
The honey can be omitted and replaced with a little artificial sweetener.

1 Using a small sharp knife, trim the stalks from the figs. Make four cuts through each fig from the stalk-end, cutting them almost through but being careful to leave them joined at the base.

2 Place the figs on serving plates and open them out.

3 In a bowl, mix together the ricotta cheese, crème fraîche, honey and vanilla essence.

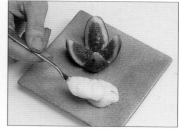

4 Spoon a little ricotta cream mixture on to each plate and sprinkle with grated nutmeg to serve.

NUTRITIONAL NOTES
Per portion:

Energy	97Kcals/405kJ
Fat, total	5.0g
Saturated fat	3.04g
Cholesterol	26.2mg
Fibre	0.8g

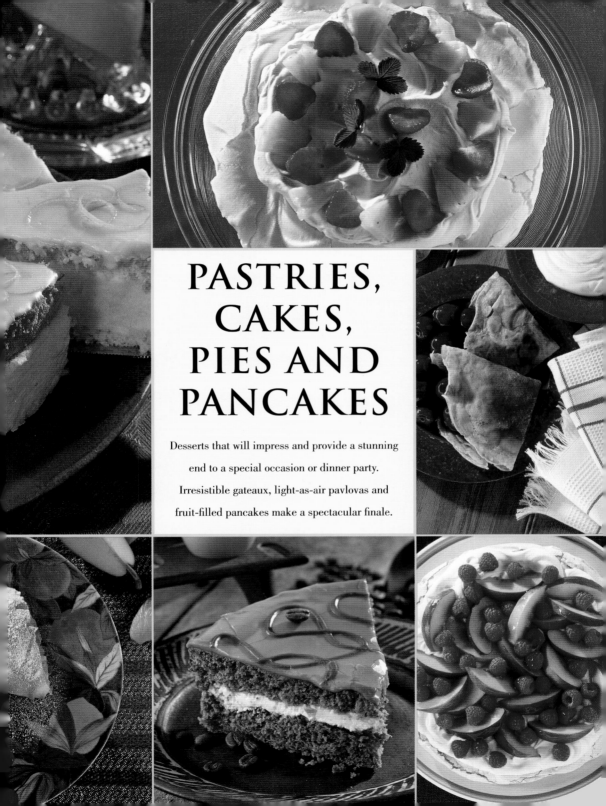

PASTRIES, CAKES, PIES AND PANCAKES

Desserts that will impress and provide a stunning
end to a special occasion or dinner party.
Irresistible gateaux, light-as-air pavlovas and
fruit-filled pancakes make a spectacular finale.

SPICED MANGO FILO FINGERS

**Mangoes have a wonderful texture and look great simply sliced and fanned out
next to these crunchy filo fingers.**

INGREDIENTS
4 mangoes
6 filo pastry sheets
90g/3½oz/7 tbsp butter, melted
45g/3 tbsp soft light brown sugar
20ml/4 tsp ground cinnamon
icing sugar, for dusting

SERVES 8

1 Preheat the oven to 200°C/400°F/Gas 6.
Set the most perfect mango aside for the
decoration. Peel the remaining mangoes
and slice the flesh. Cut the flesh across
into 3mm/⅛in thick slices.

2 Keeping the rest of the filo covered with
a damp dish towel, lay one sheet on a
baking sheet and brush with melted
butter. Mix the brown sugar and
cinnamon together and sprinkle one-fifth
of the mixture over the filo. Lay another
sheet of filo on top and repeat for the
other 5 sheets, ending with a filo sheet.

NUTRITIONAL NOTES
Per portion:

Energy	207Kcals/861kJ
Fat, total	5.0g
Saturated fat	2.75g
Cholesterol	11.5mg
Fibre	3.6g

3 Brush the top filo sheet with butter,
trim off the excess pastry and lay the
sliced mango in neat rows across the
layered filo, to cover it completely.
Brush with reserved butter and bake for
30 minutes. Allow to cool on the baking
tray, then cut into fingers.

4 Slice the flesh from either side of the
stone of the reserved mango. Cut each
piece in half lengthways. Make four long
cuts, almost to the end, in each quarter.
Dust with icing sugar. Put on a plate and
carefully fan out the slices. Serve with the
mango fingers.

FILO RHUBARB CHIFFON PIE

Filo pastry is low in fat and is very easy to bake. Keep a pack in the freezer, ready to make
impressive puddings like this one.

INGREDIENTS
500g/1¼ lb pink rhubarb
5ml/1 tsp mixed spice
finely grated rind and juice of 1 orange
15ml/1 tbsp granulated sugar
15ml/1 tbsp low-fat spread
3 sheets filo pastry, thawed if frozen

SERVES 3

VARIATION
Other fruit such as apples, pears or
peaches can be used in this pie – try it
with whatever is in season.

1 Preheat the oven to 200°C/400°F/
Gas 6. Trim the leaves and ends from
the rhubarb sticks and chop them in
2.5cm/1in pieces. Place them in a
medium-sized mixing bowl.

2 Add the mixed spice, orange rind and
juice and sugar; toss well to coat evenly.
Tip the rhubarb into a 1 litre/1¾ pint/
4 cup pie dish.

3 Melt the spread and brush over the filo
sheets. Crumple the filo loosely and place
the pieces on top of the filling to cover.

4 Place the dish on a baking sheet and
bake the pie for 20 minutes, until golden
brown. Reduce the heat to 180°C/350°F/
Gas 4 and bake for 10–15 minutes more
until the rhubarb is tender. Serve warm.

NUTRITIONAL NOTES
Per portion:

Energy	118Kcals/494kJ
Fat, total	3g
Saturated fat	0.65g
Cholesterol	0.3mg
Fibre	2.4g

APRICOT AND PEAR FILO ROULADE

This is a very quick way of making a strudel – normally, very time consuming to do –
it tastes delicious all the same!

INGREDIENTS

115g/4oz/1/2 cup ready-to-eat dried
apricots, chopped
30ml/2 tbsp apricot conserve
5ml/1 tsp lemon juice
50g/2oz/1/3 cup soft light brown sugar
2 pears, peeled, cored and chopped
30ml/2 tbsp flaked almonds
30ml/2 tbsp low-fat spread, melted
8 sheets filo pastry, thawed if frozen
5ml/1 tsp icing sugar, for dusting

SERVES 6

1 Put the apricots, apricot conserve,
lemon juice, brown sugar and pears into
a pan and heat for 5–7 minutes.

2 Remove from the heat and cool. Mix in
the flaked almonds. Preheat the oven to
200°C/400°F/Gas 6. Melt the low-fat
spread completely.

3 Lightly grease a baking sheet. Layer
the pastry on the baking sheet, brushing
each layer with the melted spread.

4 Spoon the filling down the filo, keeping
it to one side of the centre and within
2.5cm/1in of each end. Lift the other
side of the pastry up by sliding a palette
knife underneath.

5 Fold this pastry over the filling, tucking
the edge under. Seal the ends neatly and
brush all over with spread again. Bake
for 15–20 minutes, until golden. Dust
with icing sugar and serve hot, cut
into diamonds.

NUTRITIONAL NOTES	
Per portion:	
Energy	190Kcals/794kJ
Fat, total	4.1g
Saturated fat	0.54g
Cholesterol	0.1mg
Fibre	2.6g

APRICOT PARCELS

These little filo parcels contain a special apricot and mincemeat filling. A good way to use up any mincemeat and marzipan that have been in your cupboard since Christmas!

NUTRITIONAL NOTES
Per portion:

Energy	234Kcals/982kJ
Fat, total	4.4g
Saturated fat	1.1g
Cholesterol	3.7mg
Fibre	1.5g

2 Place an apricot half, hollow up, in the centre of each pastry star. Mix together the mincemeat, crushed ratafias and marzipan and spoon a little of the mixture into the hollow in each apricot.

3 Top with another apricot half, then bring the corners of each pastry together and squeeze to make a gathered purse.

4 Place the purses on a baking sheet and brush each with a little melted spread. Bake for 15–20 minutes or until the pastry is golden and crisp. Lightly dust with icing sugar to serve.

INGREDIENTS
350g/12oz filo pastry, thawed if frozen
30ml/2 tbsp low-fat spread, melted
8 apricots, halved and stoned
60ml/4 tbsp luxury mincemeat
12 ratafias, crushed
30ml/2 tbsp grated marzipan
icing sugar, for dusting

SERVES 8

1 Preheat the oven to 200°C/400°F/Gas 6. Cut the filo into thirty-two 18cm/7in squares. Brush 4 of the squares with melted spread and stack them, giving each layer a quarter turn so that the stack acquires a star shape. Repeat to make 8 stars.

COOK'S TIP
If you have run out of mincemeat, use mixed vine fruits instead.

FILO FRUIT SCRUNCHIES

Quick and easy to make, these pastries are ideal to serve at tea-time. Eat them warm or they will
lose their crispness.

INGREDIENTS
5 apricots or plums
4 sheets filo pastry, thawed if frozen
20ml/4 tsp low-fat spread, melted
50g/2oz/¹/₃ cup demerara sugar
30ml/2 tbsp flaked almonds
icing sugar, for dusting

SERVES 6

1 Preheat the oven to 190°C/375°F/Gas 5.
Halve the apricots or plums, remove the
stones and slice the fruit. Cut the filo
pastry into twelve 18cm/7in squares. Pile
the squares on top of each other and
cover with a clean dish towel to prevent
the pastry from drying out.

2 Remove one square of filo and brush it
with melted spread. Lay a second filo
square on top, then, using your fingers,
mould the pastry into folds. Quickly make
five more scrunchies in the same way so
that the pastry does not dry out.

3 Arrange a few slices of fruit in the folds
of each scrunchie, then sprinkle
generously with the demerara sugar and
flaked almonds.

4 Place the scrunchies on a baking sheet.
Bake for 8–10 minutes until golden
brown, then loosen the scrunchies from
the baking sheet with a palette knife and
transfer to a wire rack. Dust with icing
sugar and serve at once.

NUTRITIONAL NOTES
Per portion:

Energy	132Kcals/555kJ
Fat, total	4.19g
Saturated fat	0.63g
Cholesterol	0mg
Fibre	0.67g

PLUM FILO POCKETS

Cheese-filled plums, baked in filo pastry, provide a wonderful mix of sweet and savoury tastes for the palate.

INGREDIENTS

115g/4oz/¹/2 cup low-fat soft cheese
15ml/1 tbsp light muscovado sugar
2.5ml/¹/2 tsp ground cloves
8 large, firm plums, halved and stoned
8 sheets filo pastry, thawed if frozen
sunflower oil, for brushing
icing sugar, for dusting

SERVES 4

1 Preheat the oven to 220°C/425°F/ Gas 7. Mix together the low-fat soft cheese, muscovado sugar and ground cloves to make a firm paste.

2 Sandwich the plum halves together with a spoonful of the cheese mixture. Stack the filo pastry sheets and cut into 16 pieces, each 23cm/9in square. Brush one piece with oil and place a second diagonally on top. Repeat with the rest.

3 Place a plum on each filo pastry square, lift up the sides and pinch the corners together. Place on a baking sheet. Bake for 15–18 minutes, until golden, then dust with icing sugar.

NUTRITIONAL NOTES
Per portion:

Energy	188Kcals/790kJ
Fat, total	1.87g
Saturated fat	0.27g
Cholesterol	0.29mg
Fibre	2.55g

TROPICAL FRUIT FILO CLUSTERS

These fruity filo clusters are ideal for a family treat or a dinner party dessert. They are delicious served either hot or cold, on their own or with reduced-fat cream.

INGREDIENTS
1 banana, sliced
1 small mango, peeled, stoned and diced
lemon juice, for sprinkling
1 small cooking apple, coarsely grated
6 fresh or dried dates, stoned and chopped
*50g/2oz/¹/3 cup ready-to-eat dried
pineapple, chopped*
50g/2oz/¹/3 cup sultanas
50g/2oz/¹/3 cup soft light brown sugar
5ml/1 tsp ground mixed spice
8 sheets filo pastry, thawed if frozen
30ml/2 tbsp sunflower oil
icing sugar, for dusting

SERVES 8

NUTRITIONAL NOTES
Per portion:

Energy	197Kcals/833kJ
Fat, total	3.58g
Saturated fat	0.44g
Cholesterol	0mg
Fibre	2.31g

1 Preheat the oven to 200°C/400°F/
Gas 6. Line a baking sheet with non-
stick baking paper. In a medium-sized
mixing bowl, toss the banana slices
and diced mango in lemon juice to
prevent discoloration.

2 Add the apple, dates, pineapple,
sultanas, sugar and spice to the bowl and
mix well.

3 To make each fruit cluster, cut each
sheet of filo pastry in half crossways to
make two squares/rectangles (16 pieces
in total). Lightly brush two pieces of
pastry with oil and place one on top of
the other at a 45° angle.

COOK'S TIP
To prevent filo pastry drying out and
crumbling, cover with a damp cloth
before brushing with the oil.

4 Spoon some fruit filling into the centre,
gather the pastry up over the filling and
secure with string. Place the cluster on
the prepared baking sheet and lightly
brush all over with oil.

5 Repeat with the remaining pastry
squares and filling to make a total of 8
fruit clusters. Bake for 25–30 minutes,
until golden brown and crisp.

6 Carefully snip and remove the string
from each cluster and serve hot or cold,
dusted with sifted icing sugar.

REDCURRANT FILO BASKETS

Filo pastry is crisp and light and makes a very elegant dessert. It is also low in fat and needs only a fine brushing of oil before use; a light oil such as sunflower is the best choice for this recipe.

INGREDIENTS
3 sheets filo pastry, thawed if frozen
15ml/1 tbsp sunflower oil
175g/6oz/1½ cups redcurrants
250ml/8fl oz/1 cup low-fat Greek yogurt
5ml/1 tsp icing sugar

SERVES 6

1 Preheat the oven to 200°C/400°F/Gas 6. Cut the sheets of filo pastry into eighteen 10cm/4in squares.

2 Brush each filo square very thinly with oil, then arrange three squares in each of six small patty tins, placing each one at a different angle so that they form star-shaped baskets. Bake for 6–8 minutes, until crisp and golden. Lift the baskets out carefully and leave them to cool on a wire rack.

3 Set aside a few sprigs of redcurrants on their stems for decoration and string the rest. Stir the redcurrants into the low-fat Greek yogurt.

4 Spoon the yogurt into the filo baskets. Decorate them with the reserved sprigs of redcurrants and sprinkle them with the icing sugar to serve.

NUTRITIONAL NOTES
Per portion:

Energy	80Kcals/335kJ
Fat, total	3.8g
Saturated fat	1.35g
Cholesterol	2.3mg
Fibre	1g

FILO FRUIT BASKETS

Crisp filo teamed with fruit in a strawberry yogurt cream makes a fine finish for a summer meal.

INGREDIENTS

4 large or 8 small sheets of filo pastry,
thawed if frozen
25g/1oz/5 tsp low-fat spread, melted
250ml/8fl oz/1 cup low-fat Greek yogurt
60ml/4 tbsp whole-fruit strawberry jam
15ml/1 tbsp Curaçao or other
orange liqueur
115g/4oz/1 cup seedless red grapes, halved
115g/4oz/1 cup seedless green grapes,
halved
175g/6oz/1 cup fresh pineapple cubes
225g/8oz/2 cups raspberries
30ml/2 tbsp icing sugar
6 small sprigs of fresh mint, for decorating

SERVES 6

1 Preheat the oven to 180°C/350°F/Gas 4. Grease 6 cups of a bun tin.

2 Stack the filo sheets and cut into twenty-four 12cm/4½ in squares.

NUTRITIONAL NOTES
Per portion:

Energy	207Kcals/867kJ
Fat, total	4.6g
Saturated fat	1.84g
Cholesterol	3.2mg
Fibre	1.4g

3 Lay 4 squares of pastry in each of the 6 bun tins. Press the filo firmly into the tins, rotating to make star-shaped baskets.

4 Brush the pastry baskets lightly with melted low-fat spread. Bake for 5–7 minutes, until the pastry is crisp and golden. Cool on a wire rack.

5 In a bowl, mix the yogurt with the strawberry jam and liqueur.

6 Just before serving, spoon a little of the cream mixture into each pastry basket. Top with the fruit. Sprinkle with icing sugar and decorate each basket with a small sprig of mint.

FILO-TOPPED APPLE PIE

—

With its scrunchy filo topping and only a small amount of low-fat spread, this makes a really
light and healthy dessert.

INGREDIENTS
900g/2lb Bramley or other cooking apples
75g/3oz/6 tbsp caster sugar
grated rind of 1 lemon
15ml/1 tbsp lemon juice
75g/3oz/¹/2 cup sultanas
2.5ml/¹/2 tsp ground cinnamon
4 large sheets filo pastry, thawed if frozen
30ml/2 tbsp low-fat spread, melted
icing sugar, for dusting

SERVES 6

1 Peel, core and dice the apples. Place
them in a saucepan with the caster sugar
and lemon rind. Drizzle the lemon juice
over. Bring to the boil, stir well, then cook
for 5 minutes or until the apples soften.

2 Stir in the sultanas and cinnamon.
Spoon the mixture into a 1.2 litre/2 pint/
5 cup pie dish and level the top. Leave
to cool.

NUTRITIONAL NOTES
Per portion:

Energy	199Kcals/837kJ
Fat, total	2.5g
Saturated fat	0.56g
Cholesterol	0.3mg
Fibre	1.9g

3 Preheat the oven to 180°C/350°F/Gas 4.
Place a pie funnel in the centre of the
fruit. Brush each sheet of filo with melted
low-fat spread. Scrunch up loosely and
place on the fruit to cover it completely.

4 Bake for 20–30 minutes until the filo
is golden. Dust the pie with icing sugar
before serving.

VARIATION
To make filo crackers, cut the greased
filo into 20cm/8in wide strips. Spoon a
little of the filling along one end of
each strip, leaving the sides clear. Roll
up and twist the ends to make a
cracker. Brush with more melted
low-fat spread, bake for 20 minutes.

CHINESE CHESTNUT PANCAKES
—

Thin Chinese pancakes, spread with chestnut purée and fried in the minimum of oil, make a deliciously different dessert.

INGREDIENTS

90g/3oz canned sweetened chestnut purée
15ml/1 tbsp vegetable oil, for frying
caster sugar, to serve

FOR THE PANCAKES

150g/5oz/1¼ cups plain flour, plus extra
for dusting
about 105ml/7 tbsp boiling water
2.5ml/½ tsp vegetable oil

SERVES 4

1 Make the pancakes. Sift the flour and then pour in the boiling water, stirring as you pour. Mix in the oil and knead the mixture into a dough. Cover with a damp towel and leave to stand for 30 minutes.

2 Knead the dough until smooth, then roll it out into a long "sausage", cut into eight pieces and roll each into a ball. Flatten each piece, then roll it to a 15cm/6in pancake.

NUTRITIONAL NOTES
Per portion:

Energy	192Kcals/809kJ
Fat, total	3.8g
Saturated fat	0.47g
Cholesterol	0mg
Fibre	1.8g

3 Heat an ungreased frying pan until hot, then reduce the heat to low and place the pancakes, one at a time, in the pan. Turn them when small brown spots appear on the underside. Keep under a damp cloth until all are cooked.

4 Spread about 15ml/1 tbsp of the chestnut purée over each pancake, then roll it up.

5 Heat the oil in a non-stick wok or frying pan. Add the rolls in batches and fry them briefly until golden brown, turning once.

6 Cut each pancake roll into three or four pieces and sprinkle with caster sugar. Serve immediately.

TROPICAL FRUIT PANCAKES

—

Fresh fruit, coated with a citrus and honey sauce, makes the perfect pancake filling for this light and tasty dessert.

INGREDIENTS

115g/4oz/1 cup self-raising flour
pinch of grated nutmeg
15ml/1 tbsp caster sugar
1 egg
300ml/¹/₂ pint/1¹/₄ cups skimmed milk
15ml/1 tbsp melted low-fat spread
15ml/1 tbsp fine desiccated coconut
(optional)
light sunflower spray oil for frying
icing sugar, for dusting
low-fat Greek yogurt, to serve (optional)

FOR THE FILLING

225g/8oz ripe, firm mango
2 bananas
2 kiwi fruit
1 large orange
15ml/1 tbsp lemon juice
30ml/2 tbsp unsweetened orange juice
15ml/1 tbsp clear honey

SERVES 4

1 Sift the flour, nutmeg and caster sugar into a large bowl. In a separate bowl, beat the egg lightly, then beat in most of the milk. Add to the flour mixture and beat to make a thick, smooth batter. Add the remaining milk, melted spread and coconut, if using, and continue beating until the batter is smooth and of a fairly thin, dropping consistency.

2 Spray a large non-stick frying pan with a very thin coating of oil on to the surface. Heat, then pour in a little batter to cover the pan base. Fry until golden brown, then toss or turn with a spatula.

3 Repeat Step 2 with the remaining mixture to make about eight pancakes. Dice the mango, chop the bananas and slice the kiwi fruit. Peel the orange and cut into segments.

4 Place the fruit in a bowl. Mix the lemon and orange juices and honey, then pour over the fruit.

5 Spoon a little fruit down the centre of a pancake and fold over each side. Repeat with the remaining pancakes, then dust with icing sugar and serve solo or with low-fat Greek yogurt.

NUTRITIONAL NOTES

Per portion:

Energy	303Kcals/1280kJ
Fat, total	4.7g
Saturated fat	0.98g
Cholesterol	49.9mg
Fibre	4.2g

BLUEBERRY PANCAKES

These fairly thick American-style pancakes were made popular as a breakfast option, but they are equally good as a dessert.

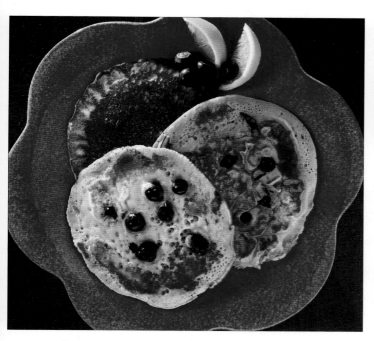

3 Heat a few drops of oil in a pancake pan or heavy-based frying pan until just hazy. Pour on about 30ml/2 tbsp of the batter and swirl it around until it makes a neat pancake.

4 Cook for 2–3 minutes. When almost set on top, sprinkle over 15–30ml/1–2 tbsp of the blueberries. As soon as the base is loose and golden brown, turn the pancake over.

5 Cook on the second side for only about 1 minute, until golden and crisp. Slide the pancake on to a plate and keep warm while you make 17 more pancakes in the same way. Serve drizzled with maple syrup, if you like, and offer lemon wedges for squeezing, if using.

INGREDIENTS
115g/4oz/1 cup self-raising flour
pinch of salt
40g/1 1/2 oz/3 tbsp caster sugar
2 eggs
120ml/4fl oz/1/2 cup skimmed milk
15ml/1 tbsp vegetable oil
115g/4oz fresh or frozen blueberries
maple syrup and miniature lemon wedges,
to serve (optional)

SERVES 6

1 Sift the flour and salt into a bowl. Add the sugar. In a separate bowl, beat the eggs thoroughly. Make a well in the middle of the flour and stir in the eggs.

COOK'S TIP
Instead of blueberries you could use fresh or thawed and drained frozen blackberries or raspberries.

2 Gradually blend in a little of the milk to make a smooth batter. Then whisk in the rest of the milk and continue to whisk for 1–2 minutes. Rest for 20–30 minutes.

NUTRITIONAL NOTES	
Per portion:	
Energy	146Kcals/618kJ
Fat, total	3.9g
Saturated fat	0.76g
Cholesterol	64.6mg
Fibre	0.9g

APPLE AND BLACKCURRANT PANCAKES

These pancakes are made with a wholewheat batter and are filled with a
delicious fruit mixture.

3 Quarter, peel and core the apples.
Slice them into a pan and add the
blackcurrants and water. Cook over a
gentle heat for 10–15 minutes until the
fruit is soft. Stir in enough demerara
sugar to sweeten.

4 Apply a light, even coat of spray oil to a
pancake pan. Heat the pan, pour in about
30ml/2 tbsp batter, swirl it around and
cook for about 1 minute. Flip the pancake
over with a palette knife and cook the
other side. Keep the pancake hot while
cooking the remaining pancakes (unless
cooking to order).

5 Fill the pancakes with the apple and
blackcurrant mixture and fold or roll
them up. Serve with a dollop of crème
fraîche, if using, and sprinkle with nuts
or sesame seeds, if you like.

INGREDIENTS
115g/4oz/1 cup wholemeal flour
300ml/¹/2 pint/1¹/4 cups skimmed milk
1 egg, beaten
15ml/1 tbsp sunflower oil
spray oil, for greasing
half-fat crème fraîche, to serve (optional)
toasted nuts or sesame seeds,
for sprinkling (optional)

FOR THE FILLING
450g/1lb Bramley or other cooking apples
225g/8oz/2 cups blackcurrants
30–45ml/2–3 tbsp water
30ml/2 tbsp demerara sugar

SERVES 4

1 Make the pancake batter. Place the
flour in a mixing bowl and make a well in
the centre.

2 Add a little of the milk with the egg
and the oil. Whisk the flour into the
liquid, then gradually whisk in the rest of
the milk, keeping the batter smooth.
Cover the batter and put it in the fridge
while you prepare the filling.

NUTRITIONAL NOTES
Per portion:

Energy	120Kcals/505kJ
Fat, total	3g
Saturated fat	0.5g
Cholesterol	25mg
Fibre	0g

CHERRY PANCAKES

These pancakes are virtually fat-free, and lower in calories and higher in fibre than traditional ones. Serve with a spoonful of natural yogurt or low-fat fromage frais.

INGREDIENTS

50g/2oz/¹/2 cup plain flour
50g/2oz/¹/2 cup wholemeal flour
pinch of salt
1 egg white
150ml/¹/4 pint/²/3 cup skimmed milk
150ml/¹/4 pint/²/3 cup water
spray oil for frying

FOR THE FILLING

425g/15oz can black cherries in syrup
7.5ml/1¹/2 tsp arrowroot

SERVES 4

1 Sift the flours and salt into a bowl, adding any bran left in the sieve to the bowl at the end. Make a well in the centre of the flour and add the egg white, then the milk and water. Beat with a wooden spoon, gradually incorporating the surrounding flour mixture, then whisk the batter hard until it is smooth and bubbly.

2 Apply a light, even coat of spray oil to a non-stick frying pan. Heat the pan, then pour in a little batter to cover the base, swirling the pan to cover the base evenly.

3 Cook until the pancake is set and golden, then turn to cook the other side. Slide on to kitchen paper and cook the remaining batter, to make 8 pancakes.

4 Drain the cherries, reserving the syrup. Mix about 30ml/2 tbsp of the syrup with the arrowroot in a saucepan. Stir in the rest of the syrup. Heat gently, stirring, until the mixture boils, thickens and clears. Add the cherries and stir until thoroughly heated. Spoon the cherries into the pancakes and fold them in quarters. Serve at once.

NUTRITIONAL NOTES

Per portion:

Energy	190Kcals/800kJ
Fat, total	1.7g
Saturated fat	0.23g
Cholesterol	0.8mg
Fibre	2.2g

SUMMER BERRY CRÊPES

—

**The delicate flavour of these fluffy crêpes contrasts beautifully
with tangy berry fruits.**

INGREDIENTS
115g/4oz/1 cup self-raising flour
1 large egg
300ml/¹/₂ pint/1¹/₄ cups skimmed milk
a few drops of pure vanilla essence
spray oil, for greasing
icing sugar, for dusting

FOR THE FRUIT
15ml/1 tbsp low-fat spread
50g/2oz/¹/₄ cup caster sugar
juice of 2 oranges
thinly pared rind of ¹/₂ orange
*350g/12oz/3 cups mixed summer berries,
such as sliced strawberries, yellow
raspberries, blueberries and redcurrants*
*45ml/3 tbsp Grand Marnier or other
orange-flavoured liqueur*

SERVES 4

1 Preheat the oven to 150°C/300°F/Gas 2.
To make the crêpes, sift the flour into a
large bowl and make a well in the centre.
Break in the egg and gradually whisk in
the milk to make a smooth batter. Stir in
the vanilla essence. Set the batter aside
in a cool place for up to half an hour.

2 Apply a light, even coat of spray oil to
an 18cm/7in non-stick frying pan. Whisk
the batter, then pour a little of it into the
hot pan, swirling to cover the base of the
pan evenly. Cook until the mixture comes
away from the sides and the crêpe is
golden underneath.

3 Flip the crêpe over with a large palette
knife and cook the other side briefly until
golden. Slide the crêpe on to a heatproof
plate. Make seven more crêpes in the
same way. Cover the crêpes with foil or
another plate and keep them hot in a
warm oven.

COOK'S TIP
For safety, when igniting a mixture for
flambéing, use a long taper or long
wooden match. Stand back as you set
the mixture alight.

4 To prepare the fruit, melt the spread in
a heavy-based frying pan, stir in the sugar
and cook gently. Add the orange juice
and rind and cook until syrupy. Add the
fruits and warm through (keeping some
back for decoration), then add the liqueur
and set it alight. Shake the pan until the
flame dies down.

5 Fold the pancakes into quarters and
arrange two on each plate. Spoon over the
fruit mixture and dust with icing sugar.
Serve the remaining fruit separately.

NUTRITIONAL NOTES
Per portion:

Energy	285Kcals/1203kJ
Fat, total	5g
Saturated fat	1.06g
Cholesterol	59.5mg
Fibre	3.5g

BLUEBERRY AND ORANGE CRÊPE BASKETS

Impress your guests with these pretty, fruit-filled crêpes. When blueberries are out of season, use other soft fruit, such as raspberries.

INGREDIENTS
150g/5oz/1¼ cups plain flour
pinch of salt
2 egg whites
200ml/7fl oz/scant 1 cup skimmed milk
150ml/¼ pint/⅔ cup orange juice
spray oil, for greasing

FOR THE FILLING
4 medium-size oranges
225g/8oz/2 cups blueberries

SERVES 6

NUTRITIONAL NOTES
Per portion:

Energy	165Kcals/697kJ
Fat, total	1.4g
Saturated fat	0.16g
Cholesterol	0.7mg
Fibre	3.2g

1 Preheat the oven to 200°C/400°F/Gas 6. Sift the flour and salt into a bowl. Make a well in the centre and add the egg whites, milk and orange juice. Beat the liquid, gradually incorporating the surrounding flour mixture, then whisk the batter until it is smooth and bubbly.

2 Apply a light, even coat of spray oil to a heavy or non-stick pancake pan and heat it. Pour in just enough batter to cover the base of the pan, swirling it to cover the pan evenly.

3 Cook until the pancake has set and is golden, and then turn it to cook on the other side. Slide the pancake on to a sheet of kitchen paper. Cook the remaining batter, to make six pancakes.

4 Invert six small ovenproof bowls or moulds on a baking sheet and drape a pancake over each. Bake them in the oven for about 10 minutes, until they are crisp and set into shape. Carefully lift the "baskets" off the moulds.

5 Pare a thin piece of orange rind from one orange and cut it in fine strips. Blanch the strips in boiling water for 30 seconds, rinse them in cold water and drain them on kitchen paper. Cut all the peel and white pith from all the oranges.

6 Cut the oranges into segments, working over a bowl to catch the juice. Add the segments and juice to the blueberries in a pan and warm gently. Spoon the fruit into the baskets and scatter the shreds of rind over the top.

COOK'S TIP
Don't fill the pancake baskets until you are ready to serve them, because they will absorb the fruit juice and begin to soften.

BANANA, MAPLE AND LIME PANCAKES

—

Pancakes are a treat any day of the week, and they can be made in advance and
stored in the freezer for convenience.

INGREDIENTS
115g/4oz/1 cup plain flour
1 egg white
250ml/8fl oz/1 cup skimmed milk
60ml/4 tbsp cold water
spray oil, for frying
shreds of lime rind, to decorate

FOR THE FILLING
4 bananas, sliced
45ml/3 tbsp maple syrup or golden syrup
30ml/2 tbsp fresh lime juice

SERVES 4

1 Make the pancake batter by beating
together the flour, egg white, milk and
water in a bowl until smooth and bubbly.
Cover and chill until needed.

2 Apply a light, even coat of spray oil to a
non-stick frying pan. Heat the pan, then
pour in a little batter to coat the base.
Swirl it around the pan to coat evenly.

3 Cook the pancake until golden, then
toss and cook the other side. Slide on to a
plate, cover with foil and keep hot while
making the remaining seven pancakes.

4 Make the filling. Mix the bananas,
syrup and lime juice in a pan and simmer
gently for 1 minute. Spoon into the
pancakes and fold into quarters. Sprinkle
with shreds of lime rind to decorate.

NUTRITIONAL NOTES
Per portion:

Energy	282Kcals/1185kJ
Fat, total	2.79g
Saturated fat	0.47g
Cholesterol	1.25mg
Fibre	2.12g

COOK'S TIP
Pancakes freeze well. To store for later
use, interleave them with non-stick
baking paper, wrap and freeze for
up to 3 months.

PINEAPPLE AND STRAWBERRY MERINGUE

This is a gooey meringue that doesn't usually hold a perfect shape, but it has a wonderful marshmallow texture.

INGREDIENTS

5 egg whites, at room temperature
pinch of salt
5ml/1 tsp cornflour
15ml/1 tbsp distilled malt vinegar
few drops of vanilla essence
275g/10oz/1 1/4 cups caster sugar
250ml/8fl oz/1 cup low-fat Greek yogurt
175g/6oz fresh pineapple, cut into chunks
175g/6oz/1 1/3 cups fresh strawberries, halved
strawberry leaves, to decorate (optional)

SERVES 6

1 Preheat the oven to 160°C/325°F/Gas 3. Line a baking sheet with non-stick baking paper.

2 Whisk the egg whites in a large grease-free bowl until they hold stiff peaks. Add the salt, cornflour, vinegar and vanilla essence; whisk again until stiff.

NUTRITIONAL NOTES

Per portion:

Energy	247Kcals/1050kJ
Fat, total	2.2g
Saturated fat	1.31g
Cholesterol	2.9mg
Fibre	0.7g

3 Gently whisk in half the sugar, then carefully fold in the rest. Spoon the meringue on to the baking sheet and swirl into a 20cm/8in round with the back of a large spoon.

4 Bake for 20 minutes, then reduce the oven temperature to 150°C/300°F/Gas 2 and bake for 40 minutes more.

5 While still warm, transfer the meringue to a serving plate, then leave to cool. To serve, top with Greek yogurt, pineapple chunks and halved strawberries. Decorate with strawberry leaves, if you have them.

COOK'S TIP

You can also cook this in a deep, 20cm/8in loose-bottomed cake tin. Cover the base with non-stick baking paper and grease the sides.

SOFT FRUIT PAVLOVA

There is rather a lot of sugar in meringue, but for special occasions this is the queen of desserts and a practical way of using up leftover egg whites.

INGREDIENTS

low-fat oil, for oiling
4 egg whites
175g/6oz/³/4 cup caster sugar
30ml/2 tbsp redcurrant jelly
15ml/1 tbsp rose water
300ml/¹/2 pint/1¹/4 cups low-fat
Greek yogurt
450g/1lb/4 cups mixed soft fruits, such as
blackberries, blueberries, redcurrants,
raspberries or loganberries
10ml/2 tsp sifted icing sugar
pinch salt

SERVES 4

1 Preheat the oven to 140°C/275°F/Gas 1. Oil a baking sheet. Whisk the egg whites with a pinch of salt in a spotlessly clean bowl, until they are white and stiff. Slowly add the caster sugar and keep whisking until the mixture forms stiff, glossy peaks.

NUTRITIONAL NOTES

Per portion:

Energy	302Kcals/1280kJ
Fat, total	3.9g
Saturated fat	2.37g
Cholesterol	5.3mg
Fibre	3.1g

2 Spoon the meringue into a 25cm/10in round on the baking sheet, making a slight indentation in the centre and giving it a swirled rim. Bake for 1–1¹/2 hours until the meringue is firm. Keep checking as the meringue can easily overcook and turn brown. Transfer the meringue to a serving plate.

3 Melt the redcurrant jelly in a small heatproof bowl resting in a pan of hot water. Cool slightly, then spread the jelly in the centre of the meringue. Gently mix the rose water with the low-fat Greek yogurt and spoon into the centre of the meringue. Arrange the fruits on top and dust lightly with the icing sugar.

HAZELNUT PAVLOVA

—

A hint of hazelnut gives the meringue a marvellous flavour, and provides a great contrast
to the summer fruit.

INGREDIENTS

3 egg whites
175g/6oz/³⁄4 cup caster sugar
5ml/1 tsp cornflour
5ml/1 tsp white wine vinegar
20g/³⁄4 oz/3 tbsp chopped roasted
hazelnuts
250g/9oz/1 cup low-fat soft cheese
15ml/1 tbsp fresh orange juice
30ml/2 tbsp low-fat natural yogurt
2 ripe nectarines, stoned and sliced
225g/8oz/2 cups raspberries, halved
15ml/1 tbsp redcurrant jelly, warmed

SERVES 4–6

1 Preheat the oven to 140°C/275°F/Gas 1.
Lightly grease a baking sheet. Draw a
20cm/8in circle on a sheet of non-stick
baking paper. Place pencil-side down on
the baking sheet.

2 Place the egg whites in a clean, grease-
free bowl and whisk until stiff. Add the
sugar 15ml/1 tbsp at a time, whisking
well after each addition.

3 Add the cornflour, vinegar and
hazelnuts and fold in carefully with a
large metal spoon.

4 Spoon the meringue on to the marked
circle and spread out to the edges,
making a dip in the centre.

5 Bake for about 1¼–1½ hours, until
crisp. Leave to cool completely and
transfer to a serving platter.

6 Beat the soft cheese and orange juice
together, stir in the yogurt and spoon on
to the meringue. Top with the fruit and
drizzle over the warmed redcurrant jelly.
Serve immediately.

NUTRITIONAL NOTES

Per portion:

Energy	332Kcals/1402kJ
Fat, total	4.4g
Saturated fat	0.82g
Cholesterol	0.3mg
Fibre	2.6g

NECTARINE AND HAZELNUT MERINGUES

If it's indulgence you're seeking, look no further. Sweet nectarines and yogurt paired with
crisp hazelnut meringues make a superb sweet.

INGREDIENTS
3 egg whites
175g/6oz/³/4 cup caster sugar
50g/2oz/¹/2 cup chopped hazelnuts, toasted
300ml/¹/2 pint/1¹/4 cups low-fat
Greek yogurt
15ml/1 tbsp sweet dessert wine
2 nectarines, stoned and sliced
fresh mint sprigs, to decorate

SERVES 5

VARIATIONS
Use apricots instead of nectarines if
you prefer, or you could try this with a
raspberry topping.

1 Preheat the oven to 140°C/275°F/Gas 1.
Line two large baking sheets with non-
stick baking paper. Whisk the egg whites
in a grease-free bowl until they form stiff
peaks. Gradually whisk in the caster
sugar a spoonful at a time until the
mixture forms a stiff, glossy meringue.

2 Fold in two thirds of the hazelnuts, then
spoon five large ovals on to each baking
sheet. Scatter the remaining hazelnuts
over five of the meringue ovals. Flatten
the remaining five ovals.

3 Bake the meringues for 1–1¹/4 hours
until crisp and dry, then carefully lift
them off the baking paper and cool
completely on a wire rack.

4 Mix the Greek yogurt lightly with the
dessert wine. Spoon some of this mixture
on to each of the plain meringues.
Arrange a few nectarine slices on each.
Put each meringue on a dessert plate with
a hazelnut-topped meringue. Decorate
each portion with mint sprigs and serve
the meringues immediately.

NUTRITIONAL NOTES
Per portion:

Energy	293Kcals/1236kJ
Fat, total	4.9g
Saturated fat	2.34g
Cholesterol	4.2mg
Fibre	1.4g

BLACKBERRY BROWN SUGAR MERINGUE

A brown sugar meringue looks very effective, especially when contrasted with a dark topping.

INGREDIENTS
175g/6oz/1 cup soft light brown sugar
3 egg whites
5ml/1 tsp distilled malt vinegar
2.5ml/1/2 tsp vanilla essence

FOR THE TOPPING
30ml/2 tbsp crème de cassis
350g/12oz/3 cups blackberries
15ml/1 tbsp icing sugar, sifted
300ml/1/2 pint/1 1/4 cups low-fat Greek yogurt
small blackberry leaves, to decorate (optional)

SERVES 6

1 Preheat the oven to 160°C/325°F/Gas 3. Draw a 20cm/8in circle on a sheet of non-stick baking paper, turn over and place on a baking sheet.

2 Spread out the brown sugar on a second baking sheet and dry in the oven for 8–10 minutes. Sieve to remove lumps.

3 Whisk the egg whites in a clean grease-free bowl until stiff. Add half the dried brown sugar, 15ml/1 tbsp at a time, whisking well after each addition. Add the vinegar and vanilla essence, then fold in the remaining sugar.

4 Spoon the meringue on to the circle, leaving a central hollow. Bake for 45 minutes, turn off the oven but leave the meringue in the oven with the door slightly open, until cold.

5 Make the topping. In a bowl sprinkle crème de cassis over the blackberries. Leave to macerate for 30 minutes.

6 When the meringue is cold, carefully peel off the non-stick baking paper and transfer the meringue to a serving plate. Stir the icing sugar into the low-fat Greek yogurt and spoon into the centre.

7 Top with the blackberries and decorate with small blackberry leaves, if you like. Serve at once.

NUTRITIONAL NOTES
Per portion:

Energy	199Kcals/833kJ
Fat, total	2.6g
Saturated fat	1.58g
Cholesterol	3.5mg
Fibre	1.8g

FLOATING ISLANDS IN HOT PLUM SAUCE
—

An unusual, low-fat pudding that is simpler to make than it looks. The plum sauce can be made
in advance, and reheated just before you cook the meringues.

INGREDIENTS
450g/1lb red plums
300ml/¹/2 pint/1¹/4 cups unsweetened
apple juice
2 egg whites
30ml/2 tbsp concentrated apple juice
freshly grated nutmeg

SERVES 4

1 Halve the plums and discard the
stones. Place them in a wide pan with the
unsweetened apple juice.

2 Bring to the boil, lower the heat, cover
and simmer gently for 15–20 minutes or
until the plums are tender.

3 Meanwhile, place the egg whites in a
grease-free bowl and whisk them until
they hold soft peaks.

4 Gradually whisk in the concentrated
apple juice, whisking until the meringue
holds fairly firm peaks.

5 Using a tablespoon, scoop the meringue
mixture into the gently simmering plum
sauce. You may need to cook the
"islands" in two batches.

6 Cover and allow to simmer gently for
2–3 minutes, until the meringues are just
set. Serve straight away, sprinkled with a
little freshly grated nutmeg.

COOK'S TIP
A bottle of concentrated apple juice
is a useful sweetener, but if you don't
have any, use a little honey instead.

NUTRITIONAL NOTES
Per portion:

Energy	77Kcals/324kJ
Fat, total	0.3g
Saturated fat	0g
Cholesterol	0mg
Fibre	1.7g

VARIATION
Add an extra dimension to this dessert
by using a fruit liqueur such as
Calvados, apricot brandy or
Grand Marnier instead of the
concentrated apple juice.

RASPBERRY VACHERIN

Meringue rounds filled with orange-flavoured fromage frais and fresh raspberries
make a perfect dinner-party dessert.

INGREDIENTS
3 egg whites
175g/6oz/³/4 cup caster sugar
5ml/1 tsp chopped almonds
icing sugar, for dusting
raspberry leaves, to decorate (optional)

FOR THE FILLING
175g/6oz/³/4 cup low-fat soft cheese
15ml/1 tbsp clear honey
15ml/1 tbsp Cointreau or other orange-flavoured liqueur
120ml/4fl oz/¹/2 cup low-fat fromage frais
225g/8oz/2 cups raspberries

SERVES 6

1 Preheat the oven to 140°C/275°F/Gas 1.
Draw a 20cm/8in circle on each of two
pieces of non-stick baking paper. Turn
the paper over so the marking is on the
underside and use it to line two heavy
baking sheets.

NUTRITIONAL NOTES
Per portion:

Energy	248Kcals/1041kJ
Fat, total	2.22g
Saturated fat	0.82g
Cholesterol	4mg
Fibre	1.06g

2 Whisk the egg whites in a grease-free
bowl until very stiff, then gradually whisk
in the caster sugar to make a stiff
meringue mixture.

3 Spoon the mixture on to the circles on
the prepared baking sheets, spreading
the meringue evenly to the edges.
Sprinkle one meringue round with the
chopped almonds.

4 Bake for 1¹/2–2 hours, then lift the
meringue rounds off the baking sheets, peel
away the paper and cool on a wire rack.

5 To make the filling, cream the soft
cheese with the honey and liqueur in a
bowl. Fold in the fromage frais and
raspberries, reserving three of the best
for decoration.

6 Place the plain meringue round on a
board, carefully spread with the filling
and top with the nut-covered round. Dust
with icing sugar, transfer to a serving
plate and decorate with the reserved
raspberries, and a sprig of raspberry
leaves, if you like.

COOK'S TIP
When making the meringue, whisk the
egg whites until they are so stiff that
you can turn the bowl upside-down
without them falling out.

BAKED BLACKBERRY CHEESECAKE

—

This light, low-fat cheesecake is best made with wild blackberries, but cultivated ones will do; or substitute other soft fruit, such as loganberries, raspberries or blueberries.

INGREDIENTS

low-fat spread, for greasing
175g/6oz/³/4 cup low-fat cottage cheese
150ml/¹/4 pint/²/3 cup low-fat
natural yogurt
15ml/1 tbsp wholemeal flour
25g/1oz/2 tbsp golden caster sugar
1 egg
1 egg white
finely grated rind and juice of ¹/2 lemon
200g/7oz/1³/4 cups fresh or thawed frozen
blackberries

SERVES 5

2 Place the cottage cheese in a food processor and process until smooth. Alternatively, rub it through a sieve, to obtain a smooth mixture.

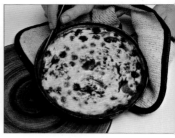

5 Run a knife around the edge of the cheesecake, and then turn it out. Remove the lining paper, and place the cheesecake on a warm serving plate.

1 Preheat the oven to 180°C/350°F/Gas 4. Lightly grease and base-line an 18cm/7in sandwich cake tin.

3 Stir in the yogurt, flour, sugar, egg and egg white. Add the lemon rind, juice and blackberries, reserving a few for decoration.

6 Decorate the cheesecake with the reserved blackberries, and serve it warm.

4 Tip the mixture into the prepared tin and bake it for 30–35 minutes, or until it is just set. Turn off the oven and leave for a further 30 minutes.

COOK'S TIP

If fresh blackberries are not in season, you can use canned blackberries. Choose those canned in natural juice and drain the fruit well before adding it to the cheesecake mixture.

NUTRITIONAL NOTES
Per portion:

Energy	95Kcals/402kJ
Fat, total	1.9g
Saturated fat	0.77g
Cholesterol	41.5mg
Fibre	1.4g

TOFU BERRY CHEESECAKE

This summery "cheesecake" makes a light and refreshing finish to any meal. Strictly speaking, it isn't a cheesecake at all, as it is based on tofu – but who would guess?

INGREDIENTS
FOR THE BASE
30ml/2 tbsp low-fat spread
30ml/2 tbsp unsweetened apple juice
115g/4oz/2½ cups bran flakes or other high-fibre cereal

FOR THE FILLING
275g/10oz/1½ cups silken tofu
250ml/8fl oz/1 cup low-fat natural yogurt
60ml/4 tbsp apple juice
15ml/1 tbsp powdered gelatine

FOR THE TOPPING
175g/6oz/1½ cups mixed summer soft fruit, such as strawberries, raspberries, redcurrants and blackberries
30ml/2 tbsp redcurrant jelly
30ml/2 tbsp hot water

SERVES 6

1 For the base, place the low-fat spread and apple juice in a pan and heat them gently until the spread has melted. Crush the cereal and stir it into the pan, mixing well. Tip into a 23cm/9in round flan tin and press down firmly. Leave to set.

2 Make the filling. Place the tofu and yogurt in a food processor and process until smooth. Pour the apple juice into a cup and sprinkle the gelatine on top. Leave until spongy, then place over hot water until melted. Stir quickly into the tofu mixture.

3 Spread the tofu mixture over the chilled base. Chill until set. Remove the flan tin and place the "cheesecake" on a serving plate.

4 Arrange the fruits over the top. Melt the redcurrant jelly with the hot water. Let it cool, then spoon over the fruit to serve.

NUTRITIONAL NOTES
Per portion:

Energy	163Kcals/688kJ
Fat, total	4.4g
Saturated fat	0.93g
Cholesterol	1.6mg
Fibre	3.2g

ANGEL CAKE

Serve this light-as-air cake with low-fat fromage frais – it makes a
perfect dessert or tea-time treat.

3 Gently fold in the flour mixture with
a large metal spoon. Spoon into an
ungreased 25cm/10in angel cake tin,
smooth the surface and bake for about
45–50 minutes, until the cake springs
back when lightly pressed.

4 Sprinkle a sheet of greaseproof paper
with caster sugar and set an egg cup in
the centre. Invert the cake tin over the
paper, balancing it carefully on the egg
cup. When cold, the cake will drop out of
the tin. Transfer it to a plate, decorate if
liked (see Cook's Tip), then dust with
icing sugar and serve.

INGREDIENTS

40g/1½ oz/⅓ cup cornflour
40g/1½ oz/⅓ cup plain flour
8 egg whites
225g/8oz/1 cup caster sugar, plus extra
for sprinkling
5ml/1 tsp pure vanilla essence
icing sugar, for dusting

SERVES 10

1 Preheat the oven to 180°C/350°F/
Gas 4. Sift both flours on to a sheet of
greaseproof paper.

2 Whisk the egg whites in a large grease-
free bowl until very stiff, then gradually
add the sugar and vanilla essence,
whisking until the mixture is thick
and glossy.

NUTRITIONAL NOTES

Per portion:

Energy	139Kcals/582kJ
Fat, total	0.08g
Saturated fat	0.01g
Cholesterol	0mg
Fibre	0.13g

COOK'S TIP

Make a lemony icing by mixing
175g/6oz/1½ cups icing sugar with
15–30ml/1–2 tbsp lemon juice. Drizzle
over the cake and decorate with physalis.

CHOCOLATE AND ORANGE ANGEL CAKE

This light-as-air sponge with its fluffy icing is virtually fat free,
yet it tastes heavenly and looks great too.

INGREDIENTS
25g/1oz/¹/4 cup plain flour
*15g/¹/2 oz/2 tbsp fat-reduced
cocoa powder*
30ml/2 tbsp cornflour
pinch of salt
5 egg whites
2.5ml/¹/2 tsp cream of tartar
115g/4oz/¹/2 cup caster sugar
*pared rind of 1 orange, blanched,
to decorate*

FOR THE ICING
200g/7oz/scant 1 cup caster sugar
75ml/5 tbsp water
1 egg white

SERVES 10

2 Add the caster sugar to the egg whites a
spoonful at a time, whisking for a few
minutes after each addition. Sift a third of
the flour and cocoa mixture over the
meringue and gently fold in with a palette
knife. Repeat the procedure, sifting and
folding in the flour and cocoa mixture two
more times.

5 Whisk the egg white in a grease-free
bowl until soft peaks occur. Add the
syrup in a thin stream, whisking all the
time. Continue to whisk until the mixture
is very thick and fluffy.

6 Spread the icing over the top and sides
of the cooled cake. Sprinkle the orange
rind over the top of the cake and serve.

1 Preheat the oven to 180°C/350°F/Gas 4.
Sift the flour, cocoa powder, cornflour and
salt together three times. Beat the egg
whites in a large grease-free bowl until
foamy. Add the cream of tartar, then
whisk until soft peaks form.

3 Spoon the mixture into a non-stick
20cm/8in ring mould and level the top.
Bake for 35 minutes or until springy when
lightly pressed. Turn upside-down on to a
wire rack and leave to cool in the tin.
Carefully lift off the tin.

4 Make the icing. Put the sugar in a pan
with the water. Stir over a low heat until
dissolved. Boil until the syrup reaches a
temperature of 120°C/250°F on a sugar
thermometer, or when a drop of the syrup
makes a soft ball when dropped into a
cup of cold water. Remove from the heat.

COOK'S TIP
Make sure you do not over-beat the egg
whites. They should not be stiff but
should form soft peaks, so that the air
bubbles can expand during cooking.

NUTRITIONAL NOTES
Per portion:

Energy	153Kcals/644kJ
Fat, total	0.27g
Saturated fat	0.13g
Cholesterol	0mg
Fibre	0.25g

CINNAMON APPLE GÂTEAU

**Make this lovely cake for an autumn celebration
when apples are at their best.**

INGREDIENTS
3 eggs
115g/4oz/¹/₂ cup caster sugar
75g/3oz/³/₄ cup plain flour
5ml/1 tsp ground cinnamon

FOR THE FILLING AND TOPPING
4 large eating apples
60ml/4 tbsp clear honey
15ml/1 tbsp water
75g/3oz/¹/₂ cup sultanas
2.5ml/¹/₂ tsp ground cinnamon
350g/12oz/1¹/₂ cups low-fat soft cheese
60ml/4 tbsp low-fat fromage frais
10ml/2 tsp lemon juice
45ml/3 tbsp smooth apricot jam, warmed
fresh mint sprigs, to decorate

SERVES 8

1 Preheat the oven to 190°C/375°F/Gas 5.
Grease and line a 23cm/9in sandwich
cake tin. Place the eggs and caster sugar
in a bowl and whisk until thick and
mousse-like (when the whisk is lifted, a
trail should remain on the surface of the
mixture for at least 15 seconds).

2 Sift the flour and cinnamon over the
egg mixture and carefully fold in with a
large spoon. Pour into the prepared tin
and bake for 25–30 minutes or until the
cake springs back when lightly pressed.
Slide a palette knife between the cake
and the tin to loosen the edge, then turn
the cake on to a wire rack to cool.

3 To make the filling, peel, core and slice
three of the apples and put them in a
saucepan. Add 30ml/2 tbsp of the honey
and the water. Cover and cook over a
gentle heat for about 10 minutes until the
apples have softened. Add the sultanas
and cinnamon, stir well, replace the lid
and leave to cool.

4 Put the soft cheese in a bowl with the
remaining honey, the fromage frais and
half the lemon juice. Beat until the
mixture is smooth.

5 Halve the cake horizontally, place the
bottom half on a board and drizzle over
any liquid from the apple mixture. Spread
with two-thirds of the cheese mixture,
then top with the apple filling. Fit the top
of the cake in place.

6 Swirl the remaining cheese mixture
over the top of the sponge. Core and slice
the remaining apple, sprinkle with the
remaining lemon juice and use to decorate
the cake edge. Brush the apple with
apricot jam and decorate with mint sprigs.

NUTRITIONAL NOTES
Per portion:

Energy	244Kcals/1023kJ
Fat, total	4.05g
Saturated fat	1.71g
Cholesterol	77.95mg
Fibre	1.5g

PEACH SWISS ROLL

A feather-light sponge with a filling of peach jam – delicious at tea time
or as a dinner-party dessert to impress your friends.

INGREDIENTS
low-fat spread, for greasing
3 eggs
115g/4oz/1/2 cup caster sugar
75g/3oz/3/4 cup plain flour, sifted
15ml/1 tbsp boiling water
90ml/6 tbsp peach jam
icing sugar, for dusting (optional)

SERVES 6–8

NUTRITIONAL NOTES
Per portion:

Energy	178Kcals/746kJ
Fat, total	2.45g
Saturated fat	0.67g
Cholesterol	82.5mg
Fibre	0.33g

1 Preheat the oven to 200°C/400°F/Gas 6.
Grease a 30 × 20cm/12 × 8in Swiss roll
tin and line with non-stick baking paper.
Combine the eggs and sugar in a bowl.
Whisk until thick and mousse-like (when
the whisk is lifted, a trail should remain
on the surface of the mixture for at least
15 seconds).

2 Carefully fold in the flour with a large
metal spoon, then add the boiling water in
the same way.

3 Spoon into the prepared tin, spread
evenly to the edges and bake for about
10–12 minutes until the cake springs
back when lightly pressed.

4 Spread a sheet of greaseproof paper on
a flat surface, sprinkle it with caster
sugar, then invert the cake on top. Peel
off the lining paper.

5 Neatly trim the edges of the cake. Make
a neat cut two-thirds of the way through
the cake, about 1cm/1/2in from the short
edge nearest you.

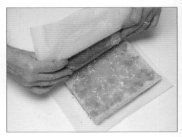

6 Spread the cake with the peach jam
and roll up quickly from the partially cut
end. Hold in position for a minute,
making sure the join is underneath. Cool
on a wire rack. Decorate with glacé icing
(see Cook's Tip) or simply dust with icing
sugar before serving.

COOK'S TIP
Decorate the Swiss roll with glacé
icing. Put 115g/4oz glacé icing in a
piping bag fitted with a small writing
nozzle and pipe lines over the top of
the Swiss roll.

APRICOT AND ORANGE ROULADE

This elegant dessert is very low in fat, so serving it with a spoonful of low-fat Greek yogurt or fromage frais would not be disastrous.

INGREDIENTS
low-fat spread, for greasing
4 egg whites
115g/4oz/¹/2 cup golden caster sugar
50g/2oz/¹/2 cup plain flour
finely grated rind of 1 small orange
45ml/3 tbsp orange juice

FOR THE FILLING
115g/4oz/¹/2 cup ready-to-eat dried apricots, roughly chopped
150ml/¹/4 pint/²/3 cup orange juice

TO DECORATE
10ml/2 tsp icing sugar, for sprinkling
shreds of pared orange rind, to decorate

SERVES 6

1 Preheat the oven to 200°C/400°F/Gas 6. Grease a 23 × 33cm/9 × 13in Swiss-roll tin and line it with non-stick baking paper. Grease the paper.

COOK'S TIP
Make and bake the sponge mixture a day in advance and keep it, rolled with the paper, in a cool place. Fill it with the fruit purée 2–3 hours before serving. The sponge can also be frozen for up to 2 months.

2 Place the egg whites in a large grease-free bowl and whisk them until they hold soft peaks. Gradually add the sugar, whisking hard after each addition.

3 Fold in the flour, orange rind and juice. Spoon the mixture into the prepared tin and spread it evenly.

4 Bake for 15-18 minutes, or until the sponge is firm and pale gold in colour. Turn out on to a sheet of non-stick baking paper, and roll it up loosely from one short side. Leave to cool.

5 Make the filling. Place the apricots in a pan, with the orange juice. Cover the pan and leave to simmer until most of the liqud has been absorbed. Purée the apricots in a food processor.

6 Unroll the roulade and spread with the apricot mixture. Roll up, arrange strips of paper diagonally across the roll, sprinkle lightly with lines of icing sugar, remove the paper and scatter with shreds of pared orange rind. Serve in slices.

NUTRITIONAL NOTES
Per portion:

Energy	154Kcals/652kJ
Fat, total	0.3g
Saturated fat	0.01g
Cholesterol	0mg
Fibre	1.5g

LEMON CHIFFON CAKE

**Lemon mousse provides a tangy filling for this light lemon sponge,
which is simple to prepare.**

INGREDIENTS
low-fat spread, for greasing
2 eggs
75g/3oz/6 tbsp caster sugar
grated rind of 1 lemon
50g/2oz/¹/2 cup plain flour, sifted
thinly pared lemon rind, cut in shreds

FOR THE FILLING
2 eggs, separated
75g/3oz/6 tbsp caster sugar
grated rind and juice of 1 lemon
30ml/2 tbsp water
15ml/1 tbsp powdered gelatine
120ml/4fl oz/¹/2 cup low-fat fromage frais

FOR THE ICING
115g/4oz/1 cup icing sugar, sifted
15ml/1 tbsp lemon juice

SERVES 8

1 Preheat the oven to 180°C/350°F/Gas 4.
Grease and line a 20cm/8in loose-
bottomed cake tin. Whisk the eggs, sugar
and lemon rind until thick and mousse-
like. Gently fold in the flour, then turn the
mixture into the prepared tin.

2 Bake for 20–25 minutes until the cake
springs back when lightly pressed in the
centre. Turn on to a wire rack to cool.
Once cold, split the cake in half
horizontally and return the lower half to
the clean cake tin. Set aside.

3 Make the filling. Put the egg yolks,
sugar, lemon rind and juice in a bowl.
Beat with a hand-held electric whisk until
thick, pale and creamy.

4 Pour the water into a small heatproof
bowel and sprinkle the gelatine on top.
Leave until spongy, then place over
simmering water and stir until dissolved.
Cool slightly, then whisk into the yolk
mixture. Fold in the fromage frais. When
the mixture begins to set, quickly whisk
the egg whites to soft peaks. Fold a
spoonful into the mousse mixture to
lighten it, then fold in the rest.

5 Pour the lemon mousse over the sponge
in the cake tin, spreading it to the edges.
Set the second layer of sponge on top and
chill until set.

6 Slide a palette knife between the tin
and the cake to loosen it, then transfer to
a serving plate. Make the icing by adding
enough lemon juice to the icing sugar to
make a mixture thick enough to coat the
back of a wooden spoon. Pour over the
cake and spread to the edges. Decorate
with the lemon rind.

NUTRITIONAL NOTES
Per portion:

Energy	202Kcals/849kJ
Fat, total	2.81g
Saturated fat	0.79g
Cholesterol	96.41mg
Fibre	0.2g

TIA MARIA GÂTEAU

A feather-light coffee sponge with a creamy liqueur-flavoured filling
and a hint of ginger to give the flavour of the Caribbean.

INGREDIENTS
low-fat spread, for greasing
75g/3oz/³⁄4 cup plain flour
30ml/2 tbsp instant coffee powder
3 eggs
115g/4oz/¹⁄2 cup caster sugar
coffee beans, to decorate (optional)

FOR THE FILLING
175g/6oz/³⁄4 cup low-fat soft cheese
15ml/1 tbsp clear honey
15ml/1 tbsp Tia Maria
50g/2oz/¹⁄4 cup stem ginger,
roughly chopped

FOR THE ICING
225g/8oz/2 cups icing sugar, sifted
10ml/2 tsp coffee essence
15ml/1 tbsp water
5ml/1 tsp cocoa powder, preferably
fat-reduced

SERVES 8

1 Preheat the oven to 190°C/375°F/
Gas 5. Grease and line a 20cm/8in deep
round cake tin. Sift the flour and coffee
powder together on to a sheet of
greaseproof paper.

2 Whisk the eggs and sugar in a bowl
until thick and mousse-like (when the
whisk is lifted, a trail should remain on
the mixture's surface for 10–15 seconds).

3 Gently fold in the flour mixture with a
metal spoon, being careful not to knock
out any air. Turn the mixture into the
prepared tin. Bake the sponge for
30–35 minutes or until it springs back
when lightly pressed. Turn on to a wire
rack and leave to cool completely.

4 Make the filling. Mix the soft cheese
with the honey in a bowl. Beat until
smooth, then stir in the Tia Maria and
the chopped stem ginger.

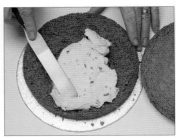

5 Split the cake in half and sandwich the
two halves with the Tia Maria filling.

6 Make the icing. Mix the icing sugar and
coffee essence with enough of the water to
make an icing that will coat the back of a
wooden spoon. Spread three-quarters of
the icing over the cake. Stir the cocoa into
the remaining icing until smooth. Spoon
into a piping bag fitted with a writing
nozzle and pipe the mocha icing over the
coffee icing. Decorate with coffee beans,
if you like.

NUTRITIONAL NOTES
Per portion:

Energy	226Kcals/951kJ
Fat, total	3.14g
Saturated fat	1.17g
Cholesterol	75.03mg
Fibre	0.64g

CUSTARDS, SOUFFLES AND WHIPS

Creamy and light yet satisfying and full of flavour,

these recipes are ideal to serve after a

rich main course to refresh the taste buds with

tantalizing flavours.

BREAD AND SULTANA CUSTARD

**An old favourite gets the low-fat treatment and proves
how successful this can be.**

INGREDIENTS

15ml/1 tbsp low-fat spread
3 thin slices of bread, crusts removed
475ml/16fl oz/2 cups skimmed milk
2.5ml/¹/₂ tsp mixed spice
45ml/3 tbsp demerara sugar
2 eggs, whisked
75g/3oz/¹/₂ cup sultanas
freshly grated nutmeg
a little icing sugar, for dusting

SERVES 4

1 Preheat the oven to 180°C/350°F/Gas 4 and lightly grease an ovenproof dish. Spread the bread with low-fat spread and cut it into small pieces.

2 Place the bread in several layers in the prepared dish.

3 Whisk together the skimmed milk, mixed spice, demerara sugar and eggs in a large mixing bowl. Pour the mixture over the bread, covering it all. Sprinkle over the sultanas and leave to stand for 30 minutes.

4 Grate a little nutmeg over the top and bake for 30–40 minutes until the custard is just set and golden. Serve sprinkled with icing sugar.

NUTRITIONAL NOTES
Per portion:

Energy	246Kcals/1037kJ
Fat, total	5g
Saturated fat	1.37g
Cholesterol	99.2mg
Fibre	0.7g

POPPYSEED CUSTARD WITH RED FRUIT

Poppyseeds add a nutty flavour to this creamy custard without increasing
the amount of fat too much.

INGREDIENTS
low-fat spread, for greasing
600ml/1 pint/2¹/2 cups skimmed milk
2 eggs
15ml/1 tbsp caster sugar
15ml/1 tbsp poppyseeds
115g/4oz/1 cup each of strawberries,
raspberries and blackberries
15ml/1 tbsp soft light brown sugar
60ml/4 tbsp red grape juice

SERVES 6

1 Preheat the oven to 150°C/300°F/Gas 2.
Grease a soufflé dish very lightly with
low-fat spread. Heat the milk until just
below boiling point, but do not boil. Beat
the eggs in a bowl with the caster sugar
and poppyseeds until creamy.

2 Whisk the milk into the egg mixture
until very well mixed. Stand the prepared
soufflé dish in a shallow roasting tin, then
pour in hot water from the kettle to come
halfway up the sides of the dish.

VARIATION
If you don't like poppyseeds,
sprinkle the surface of the custard with
freshly grated nutmeg or ground
cinnamon instead.

3 Pour the custard into the soufflé dish
and bake in the preheated oven for
50–60 minutes, until the custard is just
set and golden on top.

4 While the custard is baking, mix the
fruit with the soft brown sugar and fruit
juice. Chill until ready to serve with the
warm baked custard.

NUTRITIONAL NOTES
Per portion:

Energy	109Kcals/460kJ
Fat, total	3.1g
Saturated fat	0.69g
Cholesterol	66.2mg
Fibre	1.3g

ORANGE YOGURT BRÛLÉES

Luxurious treats, much lower in fat than classic brûlées, which are made with
cream, eggs and lots of sugar.

INGREDIENTS

2 oranges
150ml/¼ pint/⅔ cup low-fat
Greek yogurt
60ml/4 tbsp half-fat crème fraîche
45ml/3 tbsp golden caster sugar
30ml/2 tbsp light muscovado sugar

SERVES 4

1 With a sharp knife, cut away all the
peel and white pith from the oranges and
chop the fruit. Or, if there's time, segment
the oranges, removing all the membrane.

2 Place the fruit in the bottom of four
individual flameproof dishes. Mix
together the yogurt and crème fraîche and
spoon the mixture over the oranges.

3 Mix together the two sugars and
sprinkle them evenly over the tops of
the dishes.

4 Place the dishes under a preheated,
very hot grill for 3–4 minutes or until the
sugar melts and turns to a rich golden
brown. Serve warm or cold.

NUTRITIONAL NOTES
Per portion:

Energy	154Kcals/648kJ
Fat, total	3.8g
Saturated fat	2.35g
Cholesterol	15.8mg
Fibre	1.4g

TOFU BERRY BRÛLÉE

Brûlée is usually out-of-bounds on a low-fat diet, but this version is perfectly acceptable,
as it uses tofu, which is low in fat and free from cholesterol.

INGREDIENTS
300g/11oz packet silken tofu
45ml/3 tbsp icing sugar
*225g/8oz/2 cups red berry fruits, such as
raspberries, strawberries and redcurrants*
about 75ml/5 tbsp demerara sugar

SERVES 4

NUTRITIONAL NOTES
Per portion:

Energy	180Kcals/760kJ
Fat, total	3.01g
Saturated fat	0.41g
Cholesterol	0mg
Fibre	1.31g

1 Mix the tofu and icing sugar in a
food processor or blender and process
until smooth.

2 Stir in the fruits, then spoon into a
900ml/1½ pint/3¾ cup flameproof dish.
Flatten the top.

3 Sprinkle the top with enough demerara
sugar to cover evenly. Place under a
very hot grill until the sugar melts and
caramelizes. Chill before serving.

COOK'S TIP
Choose silken tofu as it gives a
smoother texture than firm tofu in this
type of dish. Firm tofu is better for
cooking in chunks.

PASSION FRUIT BRÛLÉE

Fruit brûlées are usually made with double cream, but Greek yogurt works just as well. The
brown sugar required for this recipe is reserved for the crunchy caramelized topping.

INGREDIENTS
4 passion fruit
300ml/¹/2 pint/1¹/4 cups low-fat
Greek yogurt
75g/3oz/¹/2 cup soft light brown sugar
15ml/1 tbsp water

SERVES 4

COOK'S TIP
Watch the caramel closely. It is ready
when it darkens to a rich golden brown.
At this stage it will be very hot, so
protect your hand and pour it with
great care.

1 Cut the passion fruit in half, using a
very sharp knife. Use a teaspoon to scoop
out all the pulp and seeds and divide
among four ovenproof ramekins.

2 Spoon equal amounts of the yogurt on
top of the fruit and smooth the surface
level. Chill for at least 2 hours.

3 Put the sugar in a small saucepan with
the water and heat gently, stirring, until
the sugar has melted and caramelized.
Pour over the yogurt; the caramel will
harden within 1 minute. Keep the brûlées
in a cool place until ready to serve.

NUTRITIONAL NOTES
Per portion:

Energy	139Kcals/590kJ
Fat, total	3.8g
Saturated fat	2.37g
Cholesterol	5.3mg
Fibre	0.5g

MANGO AND GINGER CLOUDS

The sweet, perfumed flavour of ripe mango combines beautifully with ginger, and this low-fat dessert makes the very most of them both.

INGREDIENTS

3 ripe mangoes

3 pieces stem ginger, plus 45ml/3 tbsp
syrup from the jar

75g/3oz/¹/2 cup silken tofu

3 egg whites

6 unsalted pistachio nuts, chopped

SERVES 6

1 Cut the mangoes' flesh off the stone, remove the peel and chop the flesh.

2 Put the mango flesh in a food processor and add the ginger, syrup and tofu. Process until smooth. Spoon into a bowl.

NOTE
Raw or lightly cooked egg whites should be avoided by women during pregnancy.

3 Whisk the egg whites in a grease-free bowl until they form soft peaks. Fold them lightly into the mango mixture.

4 Spoon the mixture into wide dishes or glasses and chill before serving, sprinkled with the chopped pistachios.

NUTRITIONAL NOTES
Per portion:

Energy	141Kcals/592kJ
Fat, total	1.9g
Saturated fat	0.21g
Cholesterol	0mg
Fibre	3.9g

RASPBERRY PASSION FRUIT SWIRLS

If passion fruit is not available, this simple dessert can be made with
raspberries alone.

2 Place alternate spoonfuls of the
raspberry pulp and the fromage frais
mixture into stemmed glasses or
serving dishes.

3 Stir lightly to create a swirled effect.
Decorate each dessert with a whole
raspberry and a sprig of fresh mint.
Serve chilled.

INGREDIENTS

300g/11oz/2½ cups raspberries
2 passion fruit
400ml/14fl oz/1⅔ cups low-fat
fromage frais
30ml/2 tbsp caster sugar
raspberries and fresh mint sprigs,
to decorate

SERVES 4

1 Using a fork, mash the raspberries in a
small bowl until the juice runs. Place the
fromage frais and sugar in a separate
bowl. Halve the passion fruit and scoop
out the seeds. Add to the fromage frais
and mix well.

COOK'S TIP

Over-ripe, slightly soft fruit can be
used in this recipe. Use frozen
raspberries when fresh are not
available, but thaw them first.

NUTRITIONAL NOTES

Per portion:

Energy	110Kcals/462kJ
Fat, total	0.47g
Saturated fat	0.13g
Cholesterol	1mg
Fibre	2.12g

CHOCOLATE VANILLA TIMBALES

You really can allow yourself the occasional chocolate treat, especially if
it's a dessert as light as this one.

INGREDIENTS

350ml/12fl oz/1¹/2 cups skimmed milk
30ml/2 tbsp cocoa powder, plus extra,
for sprinkling
2 eggs, separated
5ml/1 tsp pure vanilla essence
45ml/3 tbsp caster sugar
15ml/1 tbsp powdered gelatine
45ml/3 tbsp hot water

FOR THE SAUCE

120ml/4fl oz/¹/2 cup low-fat Greek yogurt
2.5ml/¹/2 tsp pure vanilla essence

SERVES 6

1 Mix the milk and cocoa in a pan; stir
over a moderate heat until the milk boils.
Beat the egg yolks with the vanilla and
sugar in a bowl, until smooth. Pour in the
chocolate milk, beating well.

2 Return the mixture to the pan and stir
constantly over a gentle heat, without
boiling, until it thickens slightly and is
smooth. Dissolve the gelatine in the hot
water and then quickly stir it into the
milk mixture. Let it cool until on the
point of setting.

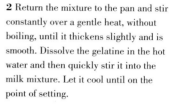

3 Whisk the egg whites in a grease-free
bowl until they hold soft peaks. Fold them
quickly into the chocolate milk mixture,
then divide among six individual moulds.
Chill until set.

4 To serve the timbales, run a knife
around the edge of each mould, dip the
moulds quickly into hot water and turn
out on to serving plates. For the sauce,
stir the yogurt and vanilla essence
together, then spoon on to the plates.
Sprinkle the sauce with cocoa powder
just before serving.

NUTRITIONAL NOTES

Per portion:

Energy	118Kcals/497kJ
Fat, total	4.1g
Saturated fat	1.89g
Cholesterol	66.7mg
Fibre	0.7g

PEACH AND GINGER PASHKA

Another low-fat version of the Russian Easter favourite – this time with peaches
and stem ginger.

INGREDIENTS
350g/12oz/1¹/₂ cups low-fat cottage cheese
2 ripe peaches or nectarines
*90g/3¹/₂oz/scant ¹/₂ cup low-fat
natural yogurt*
*2 pieces stem ginger in syrup, drained and
chopped, plus 30ml/2 tbsp syrup
from the jar*
2.5ml/¹/₂ tsp pure vanilla essence

TO DECORATE
1 peach or nectarine, peeled and sliced
10ml/2 tsp slivered almonds, toasted

SERVES 4

1 Drain the cottage cheese and rub it
through a sieve into a bowl. Stone and
roughly chop the peaches or nectarines.

2 In a bowl, mix together the chopped
peaches or nectarines, the low-fat cottage
cheese, yogurt, stem ginger, syrup and
vanilla essence.

3 Line a new, clean flower pot or a
strainer with a piece of clean, fine cloth
such as cheesecloth.

4 Tip in the cheese mixture, wrap over the
cloth and weight down. Leave over a bowl
in a cool place to drain overnight. Unwrap
the cloth and invert the pashka on to a plate.
Decorate with fruit slices and almonds.

NUTRITIONAL NOTES
Per portion:

Energy	147Kcals/621kJ
Fat, total	2.9g
Saturated fat	0.89g
Cholesterol	5.3mg
Fibre	1.1g

COOK'S TIP
Rather than making one large pashka,
line four to six cups or ramekins with
the clean cloth or muslin and divide
the mixture among them.

STRAWBERRY ROSE-PETAL PASHKA

This lighter version of a traditional Russian dessert is ideal for dinner parties – make it a day or two in advance for best results.

INGREDIENTS

350g/12oz/1¹/2 cups low-fat cottage cheese
175ml/6fl oz/³/4 cup low-fat
natural yogurt
30ml/2 tbsp clear honey
2.5ml/¹/2 tsp rose-water
275g/10oz/2¹/2 cups strawberries
handful of scented pink rose petals,
to decorate

SERVES 4

VARIATION
Use small porcelain heart-shaped
moulds with draining holes for a
pretty alternative.

---

1 Drain any free liquid from the cottage cheese and tip the cheese into a sieve. Use a wooden spoon to rub it through the sieve into a bowl. Stir the yogurt, honey and rose-water into the cheese.

2 Roughly chop about half the strawberries and fold them into the cheese mixture.

3 Line a new, clean flowerpot or a sieve with fine muslin and tip the cheese mixture in. Leave it to drain over a bowl for several hours, or overnight.

4 Invert the flowerpot or sieve on to a serving plate, turn out the pashka and lift off the muslin. Cut the remaining strawberries in half and arrange them around the pashka. Scatter the rose petals over. Serve chilled.

NUTRITIONAL NOTES

Per portion:

Energy	133Kcals/561kJ
Fat, total	1.6g
Saturated fat	1g
Cholesterol	6.1mg
Fibre	0.8g

LEMON HEARTS WITH STRAWBERRY SAUCE

These elegant little hearts are perfect for a romantic celebration, such as a
Valentine's Day dinner.

INGREDIENTS

175g/6oz/³/4 cup low-fat cottage cheese
*150ml/¹/4 pint/²/3 cup half-fat
crème fraîche*
15ml/1 tbsp granulated sugar
finely grated rind of ¹/2 lemon
30ml/2 tbsp lemon juice
10ml/2 tsp powdered gelatine
2 egg whites
low-fat spread, for greasing

FOR THE SAUCE

*225g/8oz/2 cups fresh or frozen and
thawed strawberries, plus extra to decorate*
15ml/1 tbsp lemon juice

SERVES 6

1 Press the cottage cheese through a
sieve into a bowl. Beat in the crème
fraîche, sugar and lemon rind.

2 Pour the lemon juice into a small
heatproof bowl and sprinkle the gelatine
over the surface. When it has sponged,
place the bowl over a pan of hot water and
stir to dissolve the gelatine completely.

3 Quickly stir the gelatine into the
cheese mixture, mixing it in evenly.

4 Beat the egg whites in a grease-free
bowl until they form soft peaks. Quickly
fold them into the cheese mixture.

5 Spoon the mixture into six lightly
greased, individual heart-shaped moulds,
and chill the moulds until set.

6 Make the sauce. Mix the strawberries
and lemon juice in a food processor or
blender and process until smooth. Pour
the sauce on to serving plates and invert
the lemon hearts on top. Decorate with
slices of strawberry.

COOK'S TIP

Don't worry if you haven't got heart-
shaped (coeur à la crème) moulds.
Simply use individual fluted moulds –
or even ordinary teacups.

NUTRITIONAL NOTES

Per portion:

Energy	94Kcals/397kJ
Fat, total	4.2g
Saturated fat	2.60g
Cholesterol	27.7mg
Fibre	0.4g

SOUFFLÉED RICE PUDDING

—

The fluffy egg whites in this unusually light rice pudding make the portions seem much more substantial, without adding lots of extra fat.

INGREDIENTS

65g/2¹/2 oz/¹/3 cup short-grain
(pudding) rice
45ml/3 tbsp clear honey
750ml/1¹/4 pints/3 cups
semi-skimmed milk
1 vanilla pod or 2.5ml/¹/2 tsp
vanilla essence
2 egg whites
5ml/1 tsp freshly grated nutmeg

SERVES 4

1 Place the rice, honey and milk in a heavy-based or non-stick pan and bring the milk to the boil. Add the vanilla pod, if using.

2 Lower the heat, cover and simmer over the lowest possible heat for approximately 1–1¹/4 hours, stirring occasionally to prevent sticking, until most of the liquid has been absorbed.

3 Remove the vanilla pod, or, if using vanilla essence, add this to the rice mixture now. Set the pan aside, so that the mixture cools slightly. Preheat the oven to 220°C/425°F/Gas 7.

4 Place the egg whites in a grease-free bowl and whisk them until they hold soft peaks when the whisk is lifted.

5 Using a metal spoon or spatula, fold the egg whites evenly into the rice mixture, then tip it into a 1 litre/1³/4 pint/4 cup ovenproof dish.

6 Sprinkle with grated nutmeg and bake for 15–20 minutes, until the pudding has risen well and is golden brown. Serve hot.

NUTRITIONAL NOTES
Per portion:

Energy	186Kcals/782kJ
Fat, total	3.7g
Saturated fat	1.88g
Cholesterol	13.1mg
Fibre	0g

COOK'S TIP

If you like, use skimmed milk instead of semi-skimmed, but take care when it is simmering as, with so little fat, it tends to boil over very easily.

CINNAMON AND APRICOT SOUFFLÉS

—

Don't expect this to be difficult simply because it's a soufflé – it really couldn't be easier, and, best of all, it's relatively low in fat.

INGREDIENTS
low-fat spread, for greasing
plain flour, for dusting
3 eggs
115g/4oz/¹/₂ cup apricot fruit spread
finely grated rind of ¹/₂ lemon
5ml/1 tsp ground cinnamon, plus extra
to decorate

SERVES 4

NUTRITIONAL NOTES
Per portion:

Energy	134Kcals/560kJ
Fat, total	4.1g
Saturated fat	1.15g
Cholesterol	144.4mg
Fibre	0g

1 Preheat the oven to 190°C/375°F/Gas 5. Lightly grease four individual soufflé dishes and dust them lightly with flour.

COOK'S TIP
Puréed fresh or well-drained canned fruit can be used instead of the apricot spread, but make sure that the mixture is not too wet or the soufflés will not rise properly.

2 Separate the eggs and place the yolks in a bowl with the fruit spread, lemon rind and cinnamon.

3 Whisk hard until the mixture is thick and pale in colour.

4 Place the egg whites in a grease-free bowl and whisk them until they form soft peaks when the whisk is lifted.

5 Using a metal spoon or spatula, gradually fold the egg whites evenly into the yolk mixture.

6 Divide the soufflé mixture among the prepared dishes and bake for 10–15 minutes, until well-risen and golden brown. Serve immediately, dusted with a little extra ground cinnamon.

VARIATION
Other fruit spreads would be delicious in this soufflé. Try peach or blueberry for a change.

FLUFFY BANANA AND PINEAPPLE SOUFFLÉ

This light, low-fat mousse looks very impressive but is really very easy to make, especially with a food processor.

INGREDIENTS

2 ripe bananas
225g/8oz/1 cup low-fat cottage cheese
425g/15oz can pineapple chunks or pieces in juice
60ml/4 tbsp water
15ml/1 tbsp powdered gelatine
2 egg whites

SERVES 6

1 Tie a double band of non-stick baking paper around a 600ml/1 pint/2½ cup soufflé dish, to come approximately 5cm/2in above the rim.

2 Peel and chop one banana and place it in a food processor with the cottage cheese. Process the mixture until smooth.

3 Drain the pineapple and reserve a few pieces for decoration. Add the rest of the pineapple to the mixture in the processor and process until finely chopped.

4 Pour the water into a small heatproof bowl and sprinkle the gelatine on top. Leave until spongy, then place the bowl over hot water, stirring occasionally, until all the gelatine has dissolved.

5 Whisk the egg whites in a grease-free bowl until they hold soft peaks, then fold them lightly and evenly into the mixture. Tip the mixture into the prepared dish, smooth the surface and chill it in the fridge, until set.

6 When the soufflé has set, carefully remove the paper collar. Decorate the soufflé with the reserved slices of banana and chunks of pineapple.

NUTRITIONAL NOTES
Per portion:

Energy	106Kcals/452kJ
Fat, total	0.6g
Saturated fat	0.37g
Cholesterol	1.9mg
Fibre	0.7g

HOT BLACKBERRY AND APPLE SOUFFLÉS

As the blackberry season is so short and the apple season so long, it's always worth freezing a
bag of blackberries to have on hand for treats like this one.

3 Put a spoonful of the fruit purée into
each prepared dish and smooth the
surface. Set the dishes aside.

4 Whisk the egg whites in a large grease-
free bowl until they form stiff peaks. Very
gradually whisk in the remaining caster
sugar to make a stiff, glossy meringue
mixture.

5 Fold in the remaining fruit purée and
spoon the flavoured meringue into the
prepared dishes. Level the tops with a
palette knife, and run a table knife
around the edge of each dish.

6 Place the dishes on the hot baking
sheet and bake for 10–15 minutes until
the soufflés have risen well and are lightly
browned. Dust the tops with icing sugar
and serve immediately.

INGREDIENTS
low-fat spread, for greasing
150g/5oz/²/3 cup caster sugar, plus extra
for dusting
350g/12oz/3 cups blackberries
1 Bramley or other large cooking apple,
peeled, cored and finely diced
grated rind and juice of 1 orange
3 egg whites
icing sugar, for dusting

SERVES 6

1 Preheat the oven to 200°C/400°F/Gas 6.
Grease six 150ml/¹/4 pint/²/3 cup soufflé
dishes and dust with caster sugar. Put a
baking sheet in the oven to heat.

2 Cook the blackberries and diced apple
with the orange rind and juice in a pan for
10 minutes. Press through a sieve into a
bowl. Stir in 50g/2oz/¹/4 cup of the caster
sugar. Set aside to cool.

COOK'S TIP
Running a table knife around the edge
of the soufflés before baking helps
them to rise evenly without any part
sticking to the rim of the dishes.

NUTRITIONAL NOTES
Per portion:

Energy	138Kcals/584kJ
Fat, total	0.3g
Saturated fat	0.5g
Cholesterol	0mg
Fibre	2.7g

SOUFFLÉED ORANGE SEMOLINA

If your opinion of semolina is coloured by the memory of sloppy school puddings, treat yourself
to a taste of this sophisticated version.

INGREDIENTS
50g/2oz/¼ cup semolina
600ml/1 pint/2½ cups semi-skimmed milk
30ml/2 tbsp muscovado sugar
1 large orange
1 egg white

SERVES 4

NUTRITIONAL NOTES
Per portion:

Energy	158Kcals/665kJ
Fat, total	2.67g
Saturated fat	1.54g
Cholesterol	10.5mg
Fibre	0.86g

1 Preheat the oven to 200°C/400°F/Gas 6.
Put the semolina in a non-stick pan and
add the milk and sugar. Stir over a
moderate heat until thickened and
smooth. Remove from the heat.

2 Scrub the orange rind and pare a few
long shreds of rind and save for
decoration. Finely grate the remaining
rind. Cut all the peel and white pith from
the orange and separate the flesh into
equal segments. Stir the segments into
the semolina, with the orange rind.

3 Whisk the egg white in a grease-free
bowl until stiff but not dry, then fold
lightly and evenly into the mixture. Spoon
into a 1 litre/1¾ pint/4 cup ovenproof
dish and bake for 15–20 minutes, until
risen and golden brown. Scatter over the
orange shreds and serve immediately.

COOK'S TIP
When using the rind of citrus fruit,
scrub the fruit thoroughly before use,
or buy unwaxed fruit.

QUICK APRICOT BLENDER WHIP

One of the quickest desserts you could make – and also one of the prettiest
with its delicate swirl of creamy apricot.

INGREDIENTS
400g/14oz can apricot halves in juice
15ml/1 tbsp Grand Marnier or brandy
175ml/6fl oz/3/4 cup low-fat Greek yogurt
15ml/1 tbsp flaked almonds

SERVES 4

3 Alternately spoon fruit purée and
yogurt into four tall glasses or glass
dishes, swirling them together slightly
to give a marbled effect.

4 Lightly toast the almonds until they are
golden. Let them cool slightly and then
sprinkle them on top of each whip. Serve
at once.

1 Drain the juice from the apricots and
place the fruit and liqueur in a blender
or food processor.

2 Process the apricots until smooth.

NUTRITIONAL NOTES
Per portion:

Energy	88Kcals/369kJ
Fat, total	4.4g
Saturated fat	1.38g
Cholesterol	3.1mg
Fibre	0.9g

PRUNE AND ORANGE POTS

A simple, storecupboard dessert, made in minutes. It can be served straight away, but it is best
chilled for about half an hour before serving.

INGREDIENTS
225g/8oz/1¹/2 cups ready-to-eat
dried prunes
150ml/¹/4 pint/²/3 cup orange juice
250ml/8fl oz/1 cup low-fat natural yogurt
shreds of thinly pared orange rind,
to decorate

SERVES 4

1 Remove the stones (if any), then
roughly chop the prunes. Place them
in a pan with the orange juice.

2 Bring the juice to the boil, stirring.
Lower the heat, cover and simmer for
5 minutes, until the prunes are tender
and the liquid is reduced by half.

3 Remove from the heat, allow to cool
slightly, then beat well with a wooden
spoon, until the fruit breaks down to a
rough purée.

4 Transfer the mixture to a bowl. Stir in
the yogurt, swirling the yogurt and fruit
purée together lightly, to give an
attractive marbled effect.

5 Spoon the mixture into stemmed
glasses or individual serving dishes,
smoothing the tops.

6 Top each pot with a few shreds of thinly
pared orange rind, to decorate. Chill
before serving.

COOK'S TIP
This dessert can also be made with
other ready-to-eat dried fruit, such as
apricots or peaches. If using dried
apricots, try the unsulphured variety
for a rich colour and flavour. For a
special occasion, add a dash of brandy
or Cointreau with the yogurt.

NUTRITIONAL NOTES
Per portion:

Energy	125Kcals/529kJ
Fat, total	0.7g
Saturated fat	0.28g
Cholesterol	2.3mg
Fibre	3.2g

GOOSEBERRY CHEESE COOLER

Gooseberries are one of the less common summer fruits, so they're well worth snapping up
when you can get them.

INGREDIENTS
*450g/1lb/4 cups fresh or frozen
gooseberries
1 small orange
15ml/1 tbsp clear honey
250g/9oz/1 cup low-fat cottage cheese*

SERVES 4

NUTRITIONAL NOTES
Per portion:

Energy	93Kcals/392kJ
Fat, total	1.4g
Saturated fat	0.56g
Cholesterol	3.1mg
Fibre	3.4g

1 Top and tail the gooseberries and place them in a medium-sized saucepan. Finely grate the rind from the orange and squeeze out all of the juice; then add the orange rind and juice to the pan. Cover the pan and cook gently, stirring occasionally, until the fruit is completely tender.

2 Remove from the heat and stir in the honey. Purée the gooseberries with the cooking liquid in a food processor until almost smooth. Cool.

3 Press the cottage cheese through a sieve, or process it in a food processor, until smooth. Stir half the cooled gooseberry purée into the cheese.

4 Spoon the cheese mixture into four serving dishes or glasses. Top each with a spoonful of the gooseberry purée. Serve chilled.

GRAPE CHEESE WHIPS

A deliciously cool dessert of low-fat cheese and honey, topped with
sugar-frosted grapes as decoration.

INGREDIENTS

150g/5oz/1 1/4 cups black or green seedless
grapes, plus tiny bunches
2 egg whites
15ml/1 tbsp caster sugar
finely grated rind and juice of 1/2 lemon
225g/8oz/1 cup low-fat soft cheese
45ml/3 tbsp clear honey
30ml/2 tbsp brandy (optional)

SERVES 4

NUTRITIONAL NOTES
Per portion:

Energy	135Kcals/563kJ
Fat, total	3g
Saturated fat	1.2g
Cholesterol	0.56mg
Fibre	0g

1 Brush the tiny bunches of grapes
lightly with egg white and sprinkle with
sugar to coat. Leave to dry.

2 In a bowl, mix together the lemon rind
and juice, cheese, honey and brandy if
using. Chop the remaining grapes and stir
them into the mixture.

3 Whisk the egg whites in a grease-free
bowl until stiff enough to hold soft peaks.
Fold the whites into the grape mixture,
then spoon into serving glasses.

4 Top with the sugar-frosted grapes and
serve chilled.

APRICOT DELIGHT

A fluffy mousse base with a layer of fruit jelly on top makes this dessert doubly delicious.

INGREDIENTS
*2 × 400g/14oz cans apricots in
natural juice
60ml/4 tbsp fructose
15ml/1 tbsp lemon juice
25ml/1¹/₂ tbsp powdered gelatine
425g/15oz low fat ready-to-serve custard
150ml/¹/₄ pint/²/₃ cup low-fat natural
yogurt, strained*

TO DECORATE
*1 quantity yogurt piping cream
1 apricot, sliced
1 sprig of fresh apple mint*

SERVES 8

1 Line the base of a 1.2 litre/2 pint/5 cup heart-shaped or round cake tin with non-stick baking paper.

2 Drain the apricots, reserving the juice. Put the drained apricots in a food processor or blender. Add the fructose and 60ml/4 tbsp of the apricot juice. Blend to a smooth purée.

3 Measure 30ml/2 tbsp of the apricot juice into a small bowl. Add the lemon juice, then sprinkle over 10ml/2 tsp of the gelatine. Leave for 5 minutes, until spongy.

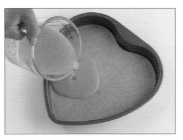

4 Stir the gelatine into half the apricot purée and pour into the tin. Chill in the fridge for 1¹/₂ hours, or until firm.

5 Sprinkle the remaining 15ml/1 tbsp gelatine over 60ml/4 tbsp of the apricot juice. Soak and dissolve as before. Mix the remaining apricot purée with the custard, yogurt and gelatine. Pour on to the layer of set fruit purée and chill in the fridge for 3 hours.

6 Dip the cake tin into hot water for a few seconds and unmould the delice on to a serving plate. Decorate with yogurt piping cream, the sliced apricot and a sprig of fresh apple mint.

COOK'S TIP
Don't use a loose-bottomed cake tin for this recipe as the mixture may seep through before it sets.

NUTRITIONAL NOTES
Per portion:

Energy	155Kcals/649kJ
Fat, total	0.63g
Saturated fat	0.33g
Cholesterol	0mg
Fibre	0.9g

FRUIT SALADS, ICES AND SORBETS

Cool, fresh and colourful – these wonderful
combinations of textures and flavours make
perfect desserts to follow spicy foods or simply to
eat on a hot, sunny afternoon.

STRAWBERRIES WITH COINTREAU

Strawberries at the height of their season are one of summer's greatest pleasures. Try this simple but unusual way of serving them.

INGREDIENTS
1 unwaxed orange
40g/1 1/2 oz/3 tbsp granulated sugar
75ml/5 tbsp water
450g/1lb/3 1/2 cups strawberries, hulled
45ml/3 tbsp Cointreau or other orange-flavoured liqueur
250ml/8fl oz/1 cup low-fat Greek yogurt

SERVES 4

1 With a vegetable peeler, remove wide strips of rind from the orange, taking care to avoid the pith. Stack two or three strips at a time and cut into very thin julienne strips.

2 Mix the sugar and water in a small saucepan. Heat gently, swirling the pan occasionally until the sugar has dissolved. Bring to the boil, add the julienne strips, then simmer for 10 minutes. Remove the pan from the heat and leave the syrup to cool completely.

3 Reserve four strawberries for decoration and cut the rest lengthways in halves or quarters. Put them in a bowl. Stir the Cointreau or chosen liqueur into the syrup and pour it over the fruit. Add the orange rind. Set aside for at least 30 minutes or for up to 2 hours.

NUTRITIONAL NOTES
Per portion:

Energy	155Kcals/653kJ
Fat, total	3.2g
Saturated fat	1.97g
Cholesterol	4.4mg
Fibre	1.2g

4 Whip the yogurt briefly, then sweeten to taste with a little of the strawberry syrup.

5 Spoon the chopped strawberries into glass serving dishes and top with dollops of the sweetened Greek yogurt. Decorate with the reserved strawberries.

FRESH FIGS WITH HONEY AND WINE

Fresh figs are naturally sweet, and they taste wonderful in a honeyed wine syrup.
Any variety can be used in this recipe, their ripeness determining the cooking time.

INGREDIENTS

450ml/¾ pint/scant 2 cups dry white wine
75g/3oz/⅓ cup clear honey
50g/2oz/¼ cup caster sugar
1 small orange
8 whole cloves
450g/1lb fresh figs
1 cinnamon stick
bay leaves, to decorate

FOR THE SAUCE

300ml/½ pint/1¼ cups low-fat
Greek yogurt
5ml/1 tsp pure vanilla essence
5ml/1 tsp caster sugar

SERVES 6

1 Put the wine, honey and sugar in a heavy-based saucepan and heat gently until the sugar dissolves.

2 Stud the orange with the cloves and add to the syrup with the figs and cinnamon. Cover and simmer until the figs are soft. Transfer to a serving dish and cool.

3 Flavour the low-fat Greek yogurt with the vanilla essence and sugar. Spoon it into a serving dish. With a small, sharp knife cut one or two of the figs in half, if you like, to show off their pretty centres. Decorate with the bay leaves and serve with the yogurt.

NUTRITIONAL NOTES

Per portion:

Energy	201Kcals/845kJ
Fat, total	2.7g
Saturated fat	1.58g
Cholesterol	3.5mg
Fibre	1.5g

PERSIAN MELON CUPS

This typical Persian dessert uses delicious, sweet fresh fruits flavoured with rose-water
and a hint of aromatic mint.

2 Reserve four strawberries and slice the rest. Place in a bowl with the melon balls, the peaches, grapes, sugar, rose-water and lemon juice.

3 Pile the fruit into the melon shells and chill in the fridge for 2 hours.

4 To serve, sprinkle with crushed ice and decorate each melon shell with a whole strawberry and a sprig of mint.

INGREDIENTS

2 small melons
225g/8oz/2 cups strawberries, sliced
3 peaches, peeled and cut into small cubes
1 bunch of seedless grapes, about 225g/8oz
30ml/2 tbsp caster sugar
15ml/1 tbsp rose-water
15ml/1 tbsp lemon juice
crushed ice
4 sprigs of mint, to decorate

SERVES 4

1 Carefully cut the melons in half and remove the seeds. Scoop out the flesh with a melon baller, taking care not to damage the skin. Reserve the melon shells for later.

COOK'S TIP

If you don't have a melon baller, scoop out the melon flesh using a large spoon and cut into bite-size pieces.

NUTRITIONAL NOTES

Per portion:

Energy	137Kcals/579kJ
Fat, total	0.4g
Saturated fat	0g
Cholesterol	0mg
Fibre	3.2g

FRAGRANT MANDARINS WITH PISTACHIOS

Mandarins, tangerines, clementines, mineolas: any of these lovely citrus fruits
could be used for this dessert.

INGREDIENTS
10 mandarins
15ml/1 tbsp icing sugar
10ml/2 tbsp orange-flower water
15ml/1 tbsp chopped pistachio nuts

SERVES 4

3 Mix the reserved mandarin juice, icing
sugar and orange-flower water and pour it
over the fruit. Cover the dish and place in
the fridge for at least an hour to chill.

4 Blanch the shreds of mandarin rind in
boiling water for 30 seconds. Drain and
cool on kitchen paper, then sprinkle them
over the mandarins, with the pistachio
nuts, to serve.

1 Pare a little of the mandarin rind and
cut into fine shreds. Squeeze the juice
from two mandarins and set it aside.

2 Peel the remaining fruit, removing all
pith. Arrange the whole fruit in a wide dish.

NUTRITIONAL NOTES
Per portion:

Energy	91Kcals/382kJ
Fat, total	2.2g
Saturated fat	0.25g
Cholesterol	0mg
Fibre	2g

ORANGE AND DATE SALAD
—

This Moroccan dessert using ingredients popular in North Africa is simplicity itself, yet it is wonderfully fresh-tasting and light at the end of a rich meal.

INGREDIENTS
6 oranges
15–30ml/1–2 tbsp orange-flower water or
rose-water (optional)
lemon juice (optional)
115g/4oz/²/₃ cup stoned dates
40g/1¹/₂ oz/scant ¹/₂ cup pistachio nuts
15ml/1 tbsp icing sugar, plus extra
for dusting
5ml/1 tsp toasted almonds

SERVES 6

3 Chop the dates and pistachio nuts and sprinkle over the salad with the icing sugar. Chill for 1 hour.

4 Just before serving, sprinkle the salad with the toasted almonds and a little extra icing sugar.

NUTRITIONAL NOTES
Per portion:

Energy	147Kcals/616kJ
Fat, total	4.3g
Saturated fat	0.45g
Cholesterol	0mg
Fibre	3.5g

1 Peel the oranges with a sharp knife, removing all the pith. Cut into segments, catching the juice in a bowl. Place in a serving dish.

2 Stir in the juice from the bowl, with a little orange-flower or rose-water, if using, and sharpen with lemon juice, if liked.

COOK'S TIP
Use fresh dates, if you can, although if you can't get hold of them dried dates are delicious in this salad, too.

FRESH FRUIT SALAD AND ALMOND CURD

Also known as Almond Float, this is a wonderfully light Chinese dessert usually made from
agar-agar or isinglass, though gelatine can also be used.

2 In a separate saucepan, dissolve the
sugar in the remaining water over the
heat. Add the milk and the almond
essence. Blend well, but do not boil.

3 Pour the agar-agar, isinglass or gelatine
mixture into a large serving bowl. Add the
flavoured milk gradually, stirring all the
time. When cool, put in the fridge for
2–3 hours to set. To serve, cut the curd
into small cubes and spoon into a serving
dish or into individual bowls. Spoon the
fruit salad over the curd and serve.

INGREDIENTS

10g/¹/4 oz agar-agar or isinglass or
25g/1oz gelatine
about 600ml/1 pint/2¹/2 cups water
50g/2oz/¹/4 cup caster sugar
300ml/¹/2 pint/1¹/4 cups semi-skimmed
milk
5ml/1 tsp almond essence
fresh fruit salad

SERVES 6

1 In a saucepan, dissolve the agar-agar
or isinglass in about half of the water
over a gentle heat. This will take at least
10 minutes. If using gelatine, follow the
instructions on the sachet.

NUTRITIONAL NOTES

Per portion:

Energy	117Kcals/499kJ
Fat, total	1.2g
Saturated fat	0.75g
Cholesterol	5.3mg
Fibre	0g

FRESH PINEAPPLE WITH COCONUT

This refreshing dessert can also be made with vacuum-packed pineapple,
and it is very simple to make and light to eat.

INGREDIENTS
1 fresh pineapple, about
675g/1 1/2 lb, peeled
few slivers of fresh coconut
300ml/1/2 pint/1 1/4 cups unsweetened
pineapple juice
60ml/4 tbsp coconut liqueur
2.5cm/1in piece stem ginger, plus 45ml/
3 tbsp syrup from the jar

SERVES 4

3 Thinly slice the stem ginger and add to
the pan with the ginger syrup. Bring just
to the boil, then simmer gently until the
liquid is slightly reduced and the sauce is
fairly thick.

4 Pour the sauce over the pineapple and
coconut, leave to cool, then chill in the
fridge before serving.

1 Peel and slice the pineapple, arrange in
a serving dish and scatter the coconut
slivers on top.

2 Place the pineapple juice and coconut
liqueur in a saucepan and heat gently.

NUTRITIONAL NOTES
Per portion:

Energy	177Kcals/743kJ
Fat, total	2.2g
Saturated fat	1.55g
Cholesterol	0mg
Fibre	2.2g

PERFUMED PINEAPPLE SALAD
—

This refreshing fruit salad benefits from being prepared ahead. This gives the fruit time to
absorb the perfumed flavour of the orange-flower water.

INGREDIENTS
1 small ripe pineapple
15ml/1 tbsp icing sugar
*15ml/1 tbsp orange-flower water, or
more if liked*
*115g/4oz/2/3 cup fresh dates, stoned
and quartered*
*225g/8oz/2 cups fresh strawberries, sliced
a few fresh mint sprigs, to serve*

SERVES 4

1 Cut the skin from the pineapple and,
using the tip of a vegetable peeler,
remove as many brown "eyes" as possible.
Quarter the pineapple lengthways,
remove the core from each wedge,
then slice.

2 Lay the pineapple slices in a shallow
glass serving bowl. Sprinkle with icing
sugar and drizzle the orange-flower
water over.

COOK'S TIP
Orange-flower water is available from
Middle Eastern food stores or good
delicatessens.

3 Add the dates and strawberries to the
pineapple, cover and chill for at least
2 hours, stirring once or twice. Serve,
decorated with a few mint sprigs.

NUTRITIONAL NOTES
Per portion:

Energy	127Kcals/534kJ
Fat, total	0.4g
Saturated fat	0g
Cholesterol	0mg
Fibre	2.9g

ICED PINEAPPLE CRUSH

The sweet tropical flavours of pineapple and lychees combine well with richly scented strawberries to make this a most refreshing salad.

INGREDIENTS
2 small pineapples
450g/1lb/4 cups strawberries
400g/14oz can lychees
45ml/3 tbsp kirsch or white rum
30ml/2 tbsp icing sugar

SERVES 4

1 Remove the crown from both pineapples by twisting sharply. Reserve the leaves for decoration.

2 Cut the fruit in half diagonally with a large serrated knife.

3 Cut around the flesh inside the skin with a small serrated knife, keeping the skin intact. Remove the core from the pineapple.

5 Combine the kirsch or rum with the icing sugar, pour over the fruit and freeze for 45 minutes.

6 Turn the fruit out into the pineapple skins and decorate with the pineapple leaves. Serve chilled.

VARIATION
You could use other tropical fruit such as mango, pawpaw or guava as well as the pineapple.

4 Chop the pineapple and combine with the strawberries and lychees, taking care not to damage the fruit.

NUTRITIONAL NOTES
Per portion:

Energy	251Kcals/1058kJ
Fat, total	0.7g
Saturated fat	0g
Cholesterol	0mg
Fibre	5.2g

COOK'S TIP
A ripe pineapple will resist pressure when squeezed and will have a sweet, fragrant smell. In winter, freezing conditions can cause the flesh to blacken.

PINEAPPLE WEDGES WITH ALLSPICE AND LIME

Fresh pineapple is easy to prepare and always looks festive, so this dish is
perfect for easy entertaining.

2 Loosen the flesh on each wedge by
sliding a knife between the flesh and the
skin. Cut the flesh into slices, leaving it
on the skin.

3 Using a canelle knife or sharp-pointed
knife, remove a few shreds of rind from
the lime. Squeeze out the juice.

INGREDIENTS

1 ripe pineapple, about 800g/1¾ lb
1 lime
15ml/1 tbsp dark muscovado sugar
5ml/1 tsp ground allspice

SERVES 4

1 Cut the pineapple lengthways into
quarters and remove the hard core from
each wedge.

4 Sprinkle the pineapple with the lime
juice and rind, sugar and allspice. Serve
immediately, or chill for up to an hour.

NUTRITIONAL NOTES

Per portion:

Energy	96Kcals/403kJ
Fat, total	0.5g
Saturated fat	0.03g
Cholesterol	0mg
Fibre	2.3g

PAPAYA AND MANGO MEDLEY WITH ICED YOGURT

Tropical fruit with iced mango yogurt makes a wonderful dessert.
Buy very ripe fruit for this dessert.

INGREDIENTS

2 large ripe mangoes, total weight
about 675g/1¹/₂ lb
300ml/¹/₂ pint/1¹/₄ cups low-fat
Greek yogurt
8 dried apricots, halved
150ml/¹/₄ pint/²/₃ cup unsweetened
orange juice
1 ripe papaya, about 300g/11oz

SERVES 4

1 Take one thick slice from one of the mangoes and, while still on the skin, slash the flesh with a sharp knife in a criss-cross pattern to make cubes.

2 Turn the piece of mango inside-out and cut away the cubed flesh from the skin. Place in a bowl, mash to a pulp with a fork, then add the Greek yogurt and mix well. Spoon into a freezer tub and freeze for about 1–1¹/₂ hours until half frozen.

3 Meanwhile, put the apricots and orange juice in a small saucepan. Bring to the boil, then simmer gently until the apricots are soft, adding a little water, if necessary, so that the apricots remain moist. Remove from the heat and set aside to cool.

4 Peel, stone and chop the remaining mangoes. Halve the papaya, remove seeds and peel. Dice the flesh and add to the mango. Pour the apricot sauce on top.

5 Stir the mango yogurt a few times. Serve the fruit topped with the mango yogurt.

NUTRITIONAL NOTES

Per portion:

Energy	231Kcals/967kJ
Fat, total	4.3g
Saturated fat	2.44g
Cholesterol	5.3mg
Fibre	7.5g

PINEAPPLE AND PASSION FRUIT SALSA

—

**Serve this fruity salsa solo or as a filling for halved baby cantaloupes.
Either way it is a cool, refreshing dessert to serve at a dinner party.**

INGREDIENTS

1 small fresh pineapple
2 passion fruit
*150ml/1/4 pint/2/3 cup low-fat
Greek yogurt*
30ml/2 tbsp light muscovado sugar
meringues, to serve (optional)

SERVES 6

1 Cut off the top and bottom of the pineapple so that it will stand firmly on a chopping board. Using a large sharp knife, slice off the peel.

2 Use a small sharp knife to carefully cut out the eyes from around the pineapple.

3 Slice the pineapple and use a small pastry cutter to stamp out the tough core from each slice. Finely chop the flesh.

4 Cut the passion fruit in half and scoop out the seeds and pulp into a bowl.

NUTRITIONAL NOTES
Per portion:

Energy	82Kcals/342kJ
Fat, total	1.5g
Saturated fat	0.79g
Cholesterol	1.8mg
Fibre	1.3g

5 Stir in the chopped pineapple and yogurt. Cover and chill.

6 Stir in the muscovado sugar just before serving the salsa. Serve with meringues, if you like.

VARIATION
Use low-fat fromage frais instead of the yogurt, if you like.

GRAPEFRUIT SALAD WITH CAMPARI AND ORANGE

The bitter-sweet flavour of Campari combines especially well with citrus fruit
for this sophisticated dessert.

INGREDIENTS

150ml/¼ pint/⅔ cup water
45ml/3 tbsp caster sugar
60ml/4 tbsp Campari
30ml/2 tbsp lemon juice
4 grapefruit
5 oranges
4 sprigs fresh mint

SERVES 4

COOK'S TIP

When buying citrus fruit, choose
brightly coloured varieties that feel
heavy for their size.

1 Bring the water to the boil in a small
saucepan, add the sugar and simmer until
dissolved. Cool in a metal tray, then add
the Campari and lemon juice. Chill until
ready to serve.

2 Peel the grapefruit and oranges.
Working over a bowl cut the fruit into
segments. Add them to the bowl, stir in
the Campari syrup and chill again.

3 Spoon the salad into four dishes and
finish with a sprig of fresh mint.

NUTRITIONAL NOTES
Per portion:

Energy	182Kcals/764kJ
Fat, total	0.4g
Saturated fat	0g
Cholesterol	0mg
Fibre	5.3g

MUSCAT GRAPE FRAPPÉ

The flavour and perfume of the Muscat grape is rarely more enticing than
when captured in this icy-cool salad.

2 Remove the seeds from the grapes with
a pair of tweezers. If you have time, peel
the grapes.

3 Scrape the frozen wine with a
tablespoon to make a fine ice. Combine
the grapes with the ice and spoon into
four shallow glasses.

INGREDIENTS

*1/2 bottle Muscat wine, Beaumes de Venise,
Frontignan or Rivesaltes*
150ml/1/4 pint/2/3 cup water
450g/1lb/4 cups Muscat grapes

SERVES 4

COOK'S TIP

To make this frappé alcohol-free,
substitute 300ml/1/2 pint/11/4 cups
apple or grape juice for the wine.

1 Pour the wine into a stainless-steel or
non-stick tray, add the water and freeze
for 3 hours or until completely solid.

NUTRITIONAL NOTES
Per portion:

Energy	155Kcals/651kJ
Fat, total	0g
Saturated fat	0g
Cholesterol	0mg
Fibre	1g

COOL GREEN FRUIT SALAD

—

**A sophisticated, simple fruit salad, which would look
wonderful served on a bed of crushed ice.**

INGREDIENTS

3 Ogen or Galia melons
115g/4oz/1 cup green seedless grapes
2 kiwi fruit
1 star fruit, plus extra slices to garnish
1 green-skinned apple
1 lime
*175ml/6fl oz/3/4 cup unsweetened
sparkling grape juice*

SERVES 6

1 Halve the melons and scoop out the
seeds. Keeping the shells intact, scoop
out the flesh and cut into bite-size cubes.
Reserve the melon shells.

2 Cut any large grapes in half. Peel and
chop the kiwi fruit. Slice the star-fruit and
set aside a few slices for decoration. Core
and slice the apple and place in a bowl,
with the other fruit.

3 Thinly pare the rind from the lime and
cut it in fine strips. Blanch the strips in
boiling water for 30 seconds, and then
drain them and rinse them in cold water.
Squeeze the juice from the lime and pour
it over the fruit. Toss lightly.

4 Spoon the prepared fruit into the
reserved melon shells; chill the shells in
the fridge until required. Just before
serving, spoon the sparkling grape juice
over the fruit and scatter with lime rind.
Decorate with slices of star fruit.

NUTRITIONAL NOTES
Per portion:

Energy	91Kcals/382kJ
Fat, total	0.4g
Saturated fat	0.00g
Cholesterol	0.0mg
Fibre	1.6g

BLACKBERRY SALAD WITH ROSE GRANITA

The blackberry is a member of the rose family and combines especially well with rose-water.
Here a rose syrup is frozen into a granita and served over strips of white meringue.

INGREDIENTS
600ml/1 pint/2¹/2 cups water
150g/5oz/²/3 cup caster sugar
petals from 1 fresh red rose, finely chopped
5ml/1 tsp rose-water
10ml/2 tsp lemon juice
450g/1lb/4 cups blackberries
icing sugar, for dusting

FOR THE MERINGUE
2 egg whites
115g/4oz/¹/2 cup caster sugar

SERVES 4

2 Preheat the oven to 140°C/275°F/Gas 1.
Line a baking sheet with six layers of
newspaper and cover with non-stick
baking paper.

4 Spoon the meringue into a piping bag
fitted with a 1cm/¹/2in plain nozzle. Pipe
the meringue in lengths across the paper-
lined baking sheet. Dry in the bottom of
the oven for 1¹/2–2 hours.

1 Bring 150ml/¹/4 pint/²/3 cup of the
water to the boil in a stainless-steel or
enamel saucepan. Add the sugar and
chopped rose petals, then lower the heat
and simmer for 5 minutes. Strain the
syrup into a deep metal tray, add the
remaining water, the rose-water and lemon
juice; leave to cool. Freeze the mixture for
approximately 3 hours or until solid.

3 Make the meringue. Whisk the egg
whites in a grease-free bowl until they
form soft peaks. Whisk in the caster
sugar, a little at a time, then continue to
whisk until the meringue forms stiff peaks
when the whisk is lifted.

5 Break the meringue into 5cm/2in
lengths and place three or four lengths
on each of four large plates. Pile the
blackberries next to the meringue. With
a tablespoon, scrape the granita finely.
Shape into ovals and place over the
meringue. Dust with icing sugar and
serve immediately.

COOK'S TIP
Serve the dessert as soon as possible
after piling the granita on the
meringue, or the meringue will soon
go soggy.

NUTRITIONAL NOTES
Per portion:

Energy	310Kcals/1318kJ
Fat, total	0.2g
Saturated fat	0g
Cholesterol	0mg
Fibre	3.5g

VARIATION
Other soft fruits such as blueberries,
raspberries or loganberries would work
equally well with this dessert.

BLUEBERRY AND ORANGE SALAD MERINGUES

What could be prettier than this simple salad composed of delicate blueberries, sharp oranges
and little meringues flavoured with lavender?

INGREDIENTS
6 oranges
350g/12oz/3 cups blueberries
8 sprigs fresh lavender

FOR THE MERINGUE
2 egg whites
115g/4oz/½ cup caster sugar
5ml/1 tsp fresh lavender flowers

SERVES 4

1 Preheat the oven to 140°/275°F/Gas 1.
Line a baking sheet with six layers of
newspaper and cover with non-stick
baking paper. Whisk the egg whites in a
large grease-free bowl until they hold soft
peaks. Add the sugar a little at a time,
whisking thoroughly after each addition.
Fold in the lavender flowers.

2 Spoon the meringue into a piping bag
fitted with a 5mm/¼ in plain nozzle. Pipe
as many small buttons of meringue on to
the prepared baking sheet as you can.
Dry the meringue near the bottom of the
oven for 1½–2 hours.

3 To segment the oranges, remove the
peel from the top, bottom and sides with a
serrated knife. Loosen the segments by
cutting with a paring knife between the
flesh and the membranes, holding the
fruit over a bowl.

4 Arrange the segments on four plates,
fanning them out.

5 Combine the blueberries with the
lavender meringues and pile in the centre
of each plate. Decorate with sprigs of
lavender and serve immediately.

NUTRITIONAL NOTES
Per portion:

Energy	198Kcals/838kJ
Fat, total	0.3g
Saturated fat	0g
Cholesterol	0mg
Fibre	3.5g

COOK'S TIP
Lavender is used in both sweet and
savoury dishes. Always use fresh or
recently dried flowers, and avoid
artificially scented bunches that are
sold for dried flower displays.

VARIATION
You could use blackberries or firm
raspberries with fresh rosemary leaves
and flowers for this dessert. You would
also make 7.5cm/3in circles of
meringue instead of small buttons
and layer the soft fruit in between
circles of meringue.

MIXED FRUIT SALAD

A really good fruit salad is always refreshing, especially when it comes bathed in fresh orange and lemon juices. Use any mixture of fresh seasonal fruits.

1 Place the fresh orange and lemon juices in a large serving bowl.

2 Prepare all the fruits by washing or peeling them as necessary. Cut them into bite-size pieces. Halve the grapes and remove any seeds. Core and slice the apples. Stone and slice soft fruits and leave small berries whole. As soon as each fruit is prepared, add it to the juices in the bowl.

3 Taste the salad, adding sugar if needed. Liqueur can also be added, if you like. Cover the bowl and put it in the fridge for at least 2 hours. Mix well before serving.

INGREDIENTS
juice of 3 large sweet oranges
juice of 1 lemon
1 banana
1–2 apples
1 ripe pear
2 peaches or nectarines
4–5 apricots or plums
115g/4oz/1 cup black or green grapes
115g/4oz/1 cup strawberries or raspberries
any other fruits in season
sugar, to taste (optional)
30–45ml/2–3 tbsp Kirsch, Maraschino or other liqueur (optional)

SERVES 4

COOK'S TIP
Try adding chopped fresh herbs such as pineapple mint, lemon balm or borage flowers, to give a herb-infused flavour to this fruit salad.

NUTRITIONAL NOTES
Per portion:

Energy	133Kcals/558kJ
Fat, total	0.4g
Saturated fat	0.03g
Cholesterol	0mg
Fibre	3.8g

SPICED FRUIT PLATTER

The spicy sour flavour of chat masala may seem a little strange at first, but this Indian dessert
can become quite addictive!

INGREDIENTS
1 pineapple
2 papayas
1 small melon
juice of 2 limes
2 pomegranates
chat masala, to taste
sprigs of fresh mint, to decorate

SERVES 6

NUTRITIONAL NOTES
Per portion:

Energy	102Kcals/429kJ
Fat, total	0.5g
Saturated fat	0g
Cholesterol	0mg
Fibre	4.8g

1 Peel the pineapple. Remove the core
and any remaining "eyes", then cut the
flesh lengthways into thin wedges. Peel
the papayas, cut them in half, and then
into thin wedges. Halve the melon and
remove the seeds from the middle. Cut it
into thin wedges and remove the skin.

2 Arrange the fruit on six individual
plates and sprinkle with the lime juice.
Cut the pomegranates in half and scoop
out the seeds, discarding any pith. Scatter
the seeds over the fruit. Serve, sprinkled
with a little chat masala to taste. Scatter
over a few sprigs of mint, to decorate.

RUBY FRUIT SALAD
—

After a rich main course, this port-flavoured fruit salad is light and refreshing.
Use any fruit that is available.

INGREDIENTS

300ml/¹/2 pint/1¹/4 cups water
115g/4oz/¹/2 cup caster sugar
1 cinnamon stick
4 cloves
pared rind of 1 orange
300ml/¹/2 pint/1¹/4 cups port
2 oranges
1 small ripe Ogen, Charentais or
honeydew melon
4 small bananas
2 dessert apples
225g/8oz/2 cups seedless grapes

SERVES 8

1 Put the water, sugar, spices and pared orange rind into a pan and stir over a gentle heat to dissolve the sugar. Then bring to the boil, lower the heat, cover and simmer for 10 minutes. Leave to cool, then add the port.

2 Strain the liquid into a bowl. With a sharp knife, cut off all the skin and pith from the oranges. Then, holding each orange over the bowl to catch the juice, cut it into segments, allowing them to drop into the syrup. Squeeze the remaining pulp to release any juice.

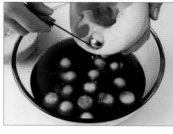

3 Cut the melon in half, remove the seeds and scoop out the flesh or cut it in small cubes. Add it to the syrup.

4 Peel the bananas and cut them diagonally in 1cm/¹/2in slices. Quarter and core the apples and cut the wedges in small cubes. Leave the skin on, or peel them if it is tough. Halve the grapes if large or leave them whole. Stir all the fruit into the syrup, cover with clear film and chill for an hour before serving.

NUTRITIONAL NOTES
Per portion:

Energy	212Kcals/895kJ
Fat, total	0.2g
Saturated fat	0.04g
Cholesterol	0mg
Fibre	1.9g

WINTER FRUIT SALAD

A colourful, refreshing and nutritious fruit salad, this makes an excellent choice
for a winter buffet.

2 Segment the oranges, catching any juice in the bowl, then add the orange segments and pineapple to the fruit juice mixture.

3 Core and chop the apples and pears and add them to the bowl.

4 Stir in the plums, dates and apricots. Cover and chill for several hours. Decorate with fresh mint sprigs to serve.

INGREDIENTS

225g/8oz can pineapple cubes in fruit juice
200ml/7fl oz/scant 1 cup fresh orange juice
200ml/7fl oz/scant 1 cup unsweetened
apple juice
30ml/2 tbsp orange- or
apple-flavoured liqueur
30ml/2 tbsp clear honey (optional)
2 oranges, peeled
2 green-skinned eating apples
2 pears
4 plums, stoned and chopped
12 fresh dates, stoned and chopped
115g/4oz/1/2 cup ready-to-eat
dried apricots
fresh mint sprigs, to decorate

SERVES 6

1 Drain the pineapple, reserving the juice in a large serving bowl. Add the orange juice, apple juice, liqueur and honey, if using, and stir.

NUTRITIONAL NOTES
Per portion:

Energy	227Kcals/967kJ
Fat, total	0.37g
Saturated fat	0g
Cholesterol	0mg
Fibre	5.34g

MIXED MELON SALAD

Several melon varieties are combined with strongly flavoured wild or
woodland strawberries for a delicious end to a meal.

INGREDIENTS
1 cantaloupe or charentais melon
1 Galia melon
900g/2lb watermelon
175g/6oz wild strawberries
4 sprigs fresh mint

SERVES 4

3 With a melon scoop, take out as many
balls as you can from all three melons.
Mix them together in a large bowl, cover
and put the bowl in the fridge. Chill for
2–3 hours.

1 Cut the cantaloupe and Galia melons
and watermelon in half.

2 Using a spoon, scoop out the seeds from
the cantaloupe and Galia.

4 Just before serving, add the wild
strawberries and mix lightly. Spoon into
four stemmed glass dishes.

5 Decorate with sprigs of mint and serve
at once.

NUTRITIONAL NOTES
Per portion:

Energy	91Kcals/381kJ
Fat, total	0.7g
Saturated fat	0g
Cholesterol	0mg
Fibre	2.7g

MARZIPAN FIGS WITH DATES

Sweet Mediterranean figs and dates combine especially well with crisp dessert apples. A hint of almond serves to unite the flavours.

INGREDIENTS
6 large apples
juice of 1/2 lemon
175g/6oz/1 cup fresh dates
25g/1oz white marzipan
5ml/1 tsp orange-flower water
60ml/4 tbsp low-fat natural yogurt
4 green or purple figs
4 almonds, toasted

SERVES 4

1 Core the apples. Slice thinly, then cut into fine matchsticks. Moisten with lemon juice to prevent them from browning.

2 Remove the stones from the dates and cut the flesh into fine strips, then mix with the apple slices in a bowl.

3 Soften the marzipan with orange-flower water and combine with the low-fat yogurt. Mix well.

4 Pile the apples and dates in the centre of four plates. Remove the stem from each of the figs and cut the fruit into quarters without slicing right through the base. Squeeze the base with the thumb and forefinger of each hand to open the fruit.

5 Place a fig in the centre of the salad, spoon in the yogurt filling and decorate each portion with a toasted almond.

NUTRITIONAL NOTES
Per portion:

Energy	210Kcals/884kJ
Fat, total	3.1g
Saturated fat	0.15g
Cholesterol	0.6mg
Fibre	5.4g

TROPICAL FRUIT SALAD

A glorious medley of tropical fruits, and ginger to add that certain spice. Like all nuts,
coconut is a significant source of fat, so go easy on the strips used for decoration.

INGREDIENTS

1 medium pineapple, about 600g/1lb 5oz
400g/14oz can guava halves in syrup
2 medium bananas, sliced
1 large mango, peeled, stoned and diced
*115g/4oz stem ginger, plus 30ml/2 tbsp of
the syrup from the jar*
60ml/4 tbsp thick coconut milk
10ml/2 tsp granulated sugar
2.5ml/¹/2 tsp freshly grated nutmeg
2.5ml/¹/2 tsp ground cinnamon
a few fine strips of coconut, to decorate

SERVES 4–6

1 Peel, core and cube the pineapple, and
place in a serving bowl. Drain the guavas,
reserving the syrup, and chop. Add the
guavas to the bowl with half the sliced
banana and the mango.

2 Chop the stem ginger and add to the
pineapple mixture.

3 Pour 30ml/2 tbsp of the ginger syrup,
and the reserved guava syrup, into a
blender or food processor. Add the
remaining banana slices with the coconut
milk and the sugar. Blend to a smooth,
creamy purée.

NUTRITIONAL NOTES
Per portion:

Energy	340Kcals/1434kJ
Fat, total	1.8g
Saturated fat	0.83g
Cholesterol	0mg
Fibre	8.1g

4 Pour the banana and coconut mixture
over the tropical fruit. Add a little grated
nutmeg and a sprinkling of cinnamon on
the top. Serve chilled, decorated with fine
strips of coconut.

MELON AND STRAWBERRY SALAD

This colourful fruit salad can be served either as a dessert or as a refreshing appetizer.
Try to find three different colours of melon to serve.

INGREDIENTS
1 Galia melon
1 honeydew melon
1/2 watermelon
225g/8oz/2 cups fresh strawberries,
halved if large
15ml/1 tbsp lemon juice
15ml/1 tbsp clear honey
15ml/1 tbsp water
15ml/1 tbsp chopped fresh mint

SERVES 4

2 Mix the lemon juice, honey and water in a jug. Pour over the fruit and mix in.

3 Sprinkle the chopped mint over the fruit and serve.

NUTRITIONAL NOTES
Per portion:

Energy	139Kcals/584kJ
Fat, total	0.84g
Saturated fat	0g
Cholesterol	0mg
Fibre	2g

1 Prepare the melons by cutting them in half and scraping out the seeds. Use a melon baller to scoop out the flesh into balls or a knife to cut it into cubes. Place these in a fruit bowl and add the fresh strawberries.

PAPAYA AND GREEN GRAPES WITH MINT SYRUP

Cool, fresh and virtually fat-free, this wonderful combination of textures and flavours makes the perfect dessert to follow a spicy main course.

INGREDIENTS
2 large papayas
225g/8oz/2 cups seedless green grapes
juice of 3 limes
2.5cm/1in fresh root ginger, peeled and finely grated
15ml/1 tbsp clear honey
5 fresh mint leaves, cut into thin strips, plus extra whole leaves, to decorate

SERVES 4

1 Peel the papaya and cut into small cubes, discarding the seeds. Cut the grapes in half.

2 In a bowl, mix together the lime juice, grated root ginger, clear honey and shredded mint leaves.

3 Add the papaya and grapes and toss well. Cover and leave in a cool place to marinate for 1 hour.

4 Serve in a large dish or individual stemmed glasses, garnished with the whole fresh mint leaves.

NUTRITIONAL NOTES
Per portion:

Energy	120Kcals/507kJ
Fat, total	0.2g
Saturated fat	0g
Cholesterol	0mg
Fibre	4.4g

PAPAYA SKEWERS WITH PASSION FRUIT COULIS

Tropical fruits, full of natural sweetness, make a simple, exotic dessert.
If you are short of time the passion fruit flesh can be used without puréeing or sieving.

INGREDIENTS

3 ripe papayas
10 passion fruit or kiwi fruit
30ml/2 tbsp fresh lime juice
30ml/2 tbsp icing sugar
30ml/2 tbsp white rum
lime slices, to garnish

SERVES 6

NUTRITIONAL NOTES
Per portion:

Energy	94Kcals/399kJ
Fat, total	0.3g
Saturated fat	0g
Cholesterol	0mg
Fibre	4.1g

3 Press the fruit pulp through a sieve placed over a bowl; discard the seeds. Add the lime juice, icing sugar and rum, then stir the coulis well until the sugar has dissolved.

4 Spoon a little coulis onto plates and place the skewers on top. Scoop the flesh from the remaining passion fruit or kiwi fruit and spoon over. Garnish with slices of lime and serve at once.

1 Cut the papayas in half and scoop out the seeds. Peel them and cut the flesh into even-size chunks. Thread the chunks on to six bamboo skewers.

2 Halve eight of the passion fruit or kiwi fruit and scoop out the flesh. Purée the flesh for a few seconds in a blender of food processor.

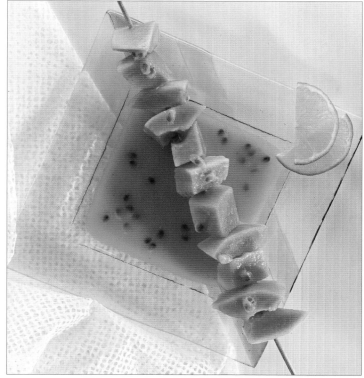

THREE-FRUIT COMPOTE

Mixing dried fruits with fresh ones makes a good combination, especially when they are flavoured delicately with a little orange-flower water.

INGREDIENTS
175g/6oz/1 cup ready-to-eat dried apricots
300ml/¹/₂ pint/1¹/₄ cups water
1 small ripe pineapple
1 small ripe melon, about 450g/1lb
15ml/1 tbsp orange-flower water
mint sprigs, to decorate

SERVES 6

NUTRITIONAL NOTES
Per portion:

Energy	86Kcals/360kJ
Fat, total	0.4g
Saturated fat	0g
Cholesterol	0mg
Fibre	3.2g

2 Peel and quarter the pineapple, then cut the core from each quarter and discard. Cut the flesh into chunks.

3 Cut the melon in half and scrape out the seeds. Working over a bowl to catch the juices, scoop balls from the flesh. Tip the juices into the apricots.

4 Put the apricots, with the soaking juices, into a bowl. Stir in the orange-flower water. Add the pineapple and melon and mix all the fruits gently.

5 Pour into a serving dish or individual dessert dishes. Decorate with a mint sprig and chill lightly before serving.

1 Put the apricots into a saucepan and pour in the water. Bring to the boil, then lower the heat and simmer for 5 minutes. Leave to cool.

VARIATION
A good fruit salad needn't consist of a mixture of fruits. For a delicious red fruit salad, try berry fruits with sliced plums, or for green fruits, try apple, kiwi fruit and green grapes.

APRICOT AND BANANA COMPOTE

This compote is delicious served on its own or with low-fat custard or ice cream. Served for breakfast, it makes a tasty start to the day.

3 Spoon the fruit and juices into a large serving dish.

4 Serve immediately, or cover and chill for several hours first. Sprinkle with flaked almonds just before serving.

INGREDIENTS

225g/8oz/1 cup ready-to-eat dried apricots
300ml/1/2 pint/1 1/4 cups unsweetened orange juice
150ml/1/4 pint/2/3 cup unsweetened apple juice
5ml/1 tsp ground ginger
3 medium bananas, sliced
25g/1oz/1/4 cup toasted flaked almonds

SERVES 4

1 Put the apricots in a saucepan with the fruit juices and ginger and stir. Cover, bring to the boil and then simmer gently for 10 minutes, stirring occasionally.

2 Set aside to cool, leaving the lid on. Once cool, stir in the sliced bananas.

COOK'S TIP

Use other combinations of dried and fresh fruit such as prunes or figs and apples or peaches.

NUTRITIONAL NOTES
Per portion:

Energy	241Kcals/1022kJ
Fat, total	4.18g
Saturated fat	0.37g
Cholesterol	0mg
Fibre	4.91g

SPICED FRUITS JUBILEE

Based on the classic Cherries Jubilee, this is a great way to use a glut of any pitted fruit. The spiced syrup is a delicious bonus.

2 Add the fruit, cover the pan and simmer for 5 minutes. Drain the fruit and set it aside; return the syrup to the pan. Boil it, uncovered, for 2 minutes or until thick and syrupy.

3 Put the arrowroot in a small bowl and stir in 30ml/2 tbsp of the brandy. Stir the mixture into the syrup. Continue cooking and stirring, until the sauce thickens. Return the fruit to the pan.

4 If serving with ice cream, place a scoop in each serving bowl and spoon the hot fruit over. Warm the remaining brandy in a small pan, then set it alight. Ladle it over the fruit at the table for maximum dramatic effect.

INGREDIENTS
115g/4oz/¹/2 cup caster sugar
thinly pared rind of 1 lemon
1 cinnamon stick
4 whole cloves
300ml/¹/2 pint/1¹/4 cups water
225g/8oz tart red plums, stoned and sliced
225g/8oz nectarines, stoned and chopped
225g/8oz/2 cups cherries, stoned
5ml/1 tsp arrowroot
75ml/5 tbsp brandy
low-fat vanilla ice cream, to serve
(optional)

SERVES 6

1 Put the sugar, lemon rind, cinnamon stick, cloves and water in a pan. Bring to the boil, stirring. Lower the heat and simmer for 5 minutes, then lift out the spices with a slotted spoon and discard.

NUTRITIONAL NOTES	
Per portion:	
Energy	151Kcals/639kJ
Fat, total	0.1g
Saturated fat	0g
Cholesterol	0mg
Fibre	1g

ITALIAN FRUIT SALAD AND ICE CREAM

If you visit Italy in the summer, you will find little pavement fruit shops selling small dishes of macerated soft fruits, which are delectable on their own, but also make a wonderful ice cream.

INGREDIENTS

900g/2lb/8 cups mixed soft fruits, such as
strawberries, raspberries, loganberries,
redcurrants, blueberries, peaches,
apricots, plums and melons
juice of 6–8 oranges
juice of 1 lemon
15ml/1 tbsp liquid pear and apple
concentrate
60ml/4 tbsp very low-fat fromage frais
30ml/2 tbsp orange-flavoured
liqueur (optional)
fresh mint sprigs, to decorate

SERVES 6

1 Prepare the fruit according to type. Cut it into reasonably small pieces, but not so small that the mixture becomes a mush.

2 Put the fruit pieces in a serving bowl and pour over enough orange juice to cover. Add the lemon juice, stir gently, cover and chill for 2 hours.

3 Set half the macerated fruit aside to serve as it is. Purée the remainder in a blender or food processor.

4 Gently warm the pear and apple concentrate and stir it into the fruit purée. Whip the fromage frais and fold it in, then add the liqueur, if using.

NUTRITIONAL NOTES

Per portion:

Energy	60Kcals/254kJ
Fat, total	0.2g
Saturated fat	0.01g
Cholesterol	0.1mg
Fibre	3.2g

5 Churn the mixture in an ice-cream maker. Alternatively, place in a container and freeze it until ice crystals form around the edge. Beat the mixture until smooth. Repeat the process once or twice, then freeze until firm. Soften slightly before serving in scoops decorated with mint accompanied by the macerated fruit.

GINGER AND HONEY SYRUP

—

Particularly good for winter puddings, this virtually fat-free sauce can be served hot or cold
with a variety of your favourite fruit salads.

INGREDIENTS
1 lemon
4 green cardamom pods
1 cinnamon stick
150ml/¼ pint/⅔ cup clear honey
3 pieces stem ginger, plus
30ml/2 tbsp syrup from the jar
60ml/4 tbsp water

SERVES 4

3 Place the lemon rind, cardamoms, cinnamon stick, honey, ginger syrup and water in a heavy-based saucepan. Boil, lower heat and simmer for 2 minutes.

4 Chop the ginger and stir it into the sauce with the lemon juice. Pour over a winter fruit salad or try it with a baked fruit compote. Chill to serve.

1 Thinly pare two strips of rind from the lemon with a potato peeler.

2 Lightly crush the cardamom pods with the back of a heavy-bladed knife. Cut the lemon in half. Reserve half for another recipe and squeeze the juice from the other half. Set the juice aside.

NUTRITIONAL NOTES
Per portion:

Energy	145Kcals/611kJ
Fat, total	0.1g
Saturated fat	0g
Cholesterol	0mg
Fibre	0g

LEMON AND LIME SAUCE

A tangy, refreshing sauce to end a heavy meal, this goes well with pancakes or fruit tarts
and is the ideal accompaniment for a rich orange or mandarin cheesecake.

2 Place all the rind in a pan, cover with
water and bring to the boil. Drain the rind
through a sieve and set it aside.

3 In a small bowl, mix a little sugar with
the arrowroot. Stir in enough water to give
a smooth paste. Heat the remaining water,
pour in the arrowroot, and stir constantly
until the sauce boils and thickens.

INGREDIENTS

1 lemon
2 limes
50g/2oz/¹/4 cup caster sugar
25ml/1¹/2 tbsp arrowroot
300ml/¹/2 pint/1¹/4 cups water
freshly made pancakes, to serve
fresh lemon balm or mint leaves, to decorate

SERVES 4

NUTRITIONAL NOTES

Per portion:

Energy	75Kcals/317kJ
Fat, total	0.1g
Saturated fat	0g
Cholesterol	0mg
Fibre	0g

1 Using a citrus zester, pare the rinds
thinly from the lemon and limes. Squeeze
the juice from the fruit.

VARIATION

This sauce can also be made with
orange and lemon rind if you prefer.

4 Stir in the remaining sugar, the citrus
juice and the reserved rind. Serve hot
with freshly made pancakes. Decorate
with lemon balm or mint.

REDCURRANT AND RASPBERRY COULIS

A dessert sauce for the height of summer to serve with light meringues and fruit sorbets.
Make it particularly pretty with a decoration of fresh flowers and leaves.

3 Blend the cornflour with the orange juice, then stir into the fruit purée. Transfer to a saucepan and bring to the boil, stirring continuously, and cook for 1–2 minutes until smooth and thick. Leave until cold.

4 Spoon the sauce over each plate. Drip the cream from a teaspoon to make small dots evenly around the edge. Draw a cocktail stick through the dots to form heart shapes. Scoop or spoon sorbet into the middle and decorate with flowers.

INGREDIENTS
225g/8oz/2 cups redcurrants
450g/1lb/4 cups raspberries
50g/2oz/1/2 cup icing sugar
15ml/1 tbsp cornflour
juice of 1 orange
30ml/2 tbsp low-fat cream
edible flowers, to decorate.

SERVES 6

1 Strip the redcurrants from their stalks. Place them in a blender with the sugar and raspberries, and blend to a purée.

2 Press the fruit mixture through a fine sieve into a bowl and discard the seeds and pulp.

NUTRITIONAL NOTES
Per portion:

Energy	81Kcals/340kJ
Fat, total	1.2g
Saturated fat	0.6g
Cholesterol	0mg
Fibre	3.2g

CHRISTMAS CRANBERRY BOMBE

This alternative to Christmas pudding is light and low in fat,
but still very festive and luxurious.

INGREDIENTS
250ml/8fl oz/1 cup buttermilk
60ml/4 tbsp low-fat crème fraîche
1 vanilla pod
2 eggs
30ml/2 tbsp clear honey
30ml/2 tbsp chopped angelica
30ml/2 tbsp mixed peel
10ml/2 tsp flaked almonds, toasted

FOR THE SORBET CENTRE
175g/6oz/1 1/2 cups fresh or
frozen cranberries
150ml/1/4 pint/2/3 cup fresh orange juice
finely grated rind of 1/2 orange
2.5ml/1/2 tsp mixed spice
50g/2oz/1/4 cup golden caster sugar

SERVES 6

1 Heat the buttermilk, crème fraîche and
vanilla pod until the mixture is almost
boiling. Remove the vanilla pod.

NUTRITIONAL NOTES
Per portion:

Energy	153Kcals/644kJ
Fat, total	4.6g
Saturated fat	1.58g
Cholesterol	75.5mg
Fibre	1.5g

2 Place the eggs in a heatproof bowl over
a pan of hot water and whisk until they
are pale and thick. Pour in the heated
buttermilk in a thin stream, whisking
hard. Continue whisking over the hot
water until the mixture thickens slightly.

3 Whisk in the honey and leave to cool.
Spoon the mixture into a freezer container
and freeze until slushy, then tip into a
bowl and stir in the chopped angelica,
mixed peel and almonds.

4 Pack into a 1.2 litre/2 pint/5 cup
pudding basin and hollow out the centre.
Freeze until firm.

5 Meanwhile, make the sorbet centre. Put
the cranberries, orange juice, rind and
spice in a pan and cook gently until the
cranberries are soft. Set some cranberries
aside for decorating. Add the sugar to the
rest, then purée in a food processor until
almost smooth, but still with some
texture. Leave to cool.

6 Fill the hollowed-out centre of the
bombe with the cranberry mixture,
smooth over and freeze until firm. To
serve, allow to soften slightly at room
temperature, then turn out and serve in
medium-sized slices, decorated with the
reserved cranberries.

SUMMER FRUIT SALAD ICE CREAM

**What could be more cooling on a hot summer day than fresh summer fruits,
lightly frozen in this irresistible ice?**

INGREDIENTS

*900g/2lb/6 cups mixed soft summer fruit,
such as raspberries, strawberries,
blackcurrants or redcurrants
2 eggs
250ml/8fl oz/1 cup low-fat Greek yogurt
175ml/6fl oz/3/4 cup red grape juice
15ml/1 tbsp powdered gelatine*

SERVES 6

1 Reserve half the fruit for the
decoration; purée the rest in a food
processor, then sieve it over a bowl to
make a smooth purée.

VARIATION

You could use other combinations of
summer fruit such as apricots, peaches
and nectarines, with apple or orange
juice for a more delicate ice-cream.

NUTRITIONAL NOTES

Per portion:

Energy	116Kcals/489kJ
Fat, total	3.9g
Saturated fat	1.69g
Cholesterol	66.8mg
Fibre	3.6g

2 Separate the eggs and whisk the yolks
and the yogurt into the fruit purée.

3 Heat the grape juice until almost
boiling, then remove it from the heat.
Sprinkle the gelatine over the grape
juice and stir to dissolve the gelatine
completely.

COOK'S TIP

Red grape juice has a good flavour and
improves the colour of the ice, but if it
is not available, use cranberry, apple or
orange juice instead.

4 Whisk the dissolved gelatine mixture
into the fruit purée. Cool, then pour the
mixture into a container that can safely
be used in the freezer. Freeze until half-
frozen and slushy in consistency.

5 Whisk the egg whites in a grease-free
bowl until stiff. Quickly fold them into the
half-frozen mixture.

6 Return the ice cream to the freezer and
freeze until almost firm. Scoop into
individual dishes and decorate with the
reserved soft fruits.

FROZEN APPLE AND BLACKBERRY TERRINE

Apples and blackberries are a classic autumn combination; they really complement each other.
This pretty, three-layered terrine can be frozen, so you can enjoy it at any time of year.

INGREDIENTS

450g/1lb cooking or eating apples
300ml/¹⁄₂ pint/1¹⁄₄ cups sweet cider
15ml/1 tbsp clear honey
5ml/1 tsp pure vanilla essence
200g/7oz/scant 2 cups fresh or frozen and thawed blackberries
15ml/1 tbsp powdered gelatine
2 egg whites
fresh apple slices and blackberries, to decorate

SERVES 6

1 Peel, core and chop the apples and place them in a pan with half the cider. Bring the cider to the boil, then lower the heat, cover the pan and let the apples simmer gently until tender.

VARIATION

For a quicker version the mixture can be set without the layering. Purée the apples and blackberries together, stir the dissolved gelatine and whisked egg whites into the mixture, turn the whole thing into the tin and leave the mixture to set.

2 Tip the apples into a food processor and process them to a smooth purée. Stir in the honey and vanilla essence. Add half the blackberries to half the apple purée, and process again until smooth. Sieve to remove the pips.

3 Heat the remaining cider until almost boiling, then sprinkle the gelatine over and stir until the gelatine has dissolved completely. Add half the gelatine mixture to the apple purée and half to the blackberry purée.

NUTRITIONAL NOTES

Per portion:

Energy	83Kcals/346kJ
Fat, total	0.2g
Saturated fat	0g
Cholesterol	0mg
Fibre	2.6g

4 Leave both purées to cool until almost set. Whisk the egg whites until they are stiff. Quickly fold them into the apple purée. Remove half the purée to another bowl. Stir the remaining whole blackberries into half the apple purée, and then tip this into a 1.75 litre/3 pint/7¹⁄₂ cup loaf tin, packing it down firmly.

5 Top with the blackberry purée and spread it evenly. Finally, add a layer of the plain apple purée and smooth it evenly. If necessary, freeze each layer until firm before adding the next.

6 Freeze until firm. When ready to serve, remove from the freezer and allow to stand at room temperature for about 20 minutes to soften. Serve in slices, decorated with fresh apple slices and blackberries.

KEY LIME SORBET

Cool and refreshing, this traditional American sorbet is ideal for serving after a curry
or similar spicy dish.

INGREDIENTS
275g/10oz/1¼ cups granulated sugar
600ml/1 pint/2½ cups water
grated rind of 1 lime
175ml/6fl oz/¾ cup fresh lime juice
15ml/1 tbsp fresh lemon juice
30ml/2 tbsp icing sugar
lime shreds, to decorate

SERVES 4

1 In a small heavy saucepan, dissolve the
granulated sugar in the water, without
stirring, over medium heat. When the
sugar has dissolved, boil the syrup for
5–6 minutes. Remove from the heat and
leave to cool.

2 Mix the cooled sugar syrup and lime
rind and juice in a jug or bowl. Stir well.
Sharpen the flavour by adding the lemon
juice. Stir in the icing sugar.

3 Freeze the mixture in an ice-cream
maker, following the manufacturer's
instructions. Decorate with lime shreds.

NUTRITIONAL NOTES
Per portion:

Energy	300Kcals/1278kJ
Fat, total	0g
Saturated fat	0g
Cholesterol	0mg
Fibre	0g

COOK'S TIP
If you do not have an ice-cream maker,
pour the mixture into a metal or plastic
freezer container and freeze until softly
set, about 3 hours. Remove from the
container and chop roughly. Process in
a food processor until smooth. Return
the mixture to the freezer container and
freeze again until set. Repeat this
process 2 or 3 times, until a smooth
consistency is obtained.

RUBY GRAPEFRUIT SORBET

On a hot day, nothing slips down more easily than a smooth sorbet.
This one looks as good as it tastes.

INGREDIENTS

175g/6oz/³/4 cup granulated sugar
120ml/4fl oz/¹/2 cup water
1 litre/1³/4 pints/4 cups strained freshly
squeezed ruby grapefruit juice
15ml/1 tbsp fresh lemon juice
15ml/1 tbsp icing sugar
mint leaves, to decorate

SERVES 8

1 In a small heavy saucepan, dissolve the granulated sugar in the water over a medium heat, without stirring. When the sugar has dissolved, boil the syrup for 3–4 minutes. Remove from the heat and leave to cool.

2 Pour the cooled sugar syrup into the grapefruit juice. Stir well. Taste the mixture and adjust the flavour by adding the lemon juice or the icing sugar, if necessary, but do not over-sweeten.

3 Pour the mixture into a metal or plastic freezer container and freeze for about 3 hours, or until softly-set.

4 Remove from the container and chop roughly into 7.5cm/3in pieces. Place in a food processor and process until smooth. Return the mixture to the freezer container and freeze again until set. Repeat this freezing and chopping process 2 or 3 times, until a smooth consistency is obtained.

5 Alternatively, freeze the sorbet in an ice-cream maker, following the manufacturer's instructions. Serve, decorated with mint leaves.

NUTRITIONAL NOTES
Per portion:

Energy	133Kcals/568kJ
Fat, total	0.1g
Saturated fat	0g
Cholesterol	0mg
Fibre	0g

MANGO SORBET WITH MANGO SAUCE
—

After a heavy meal, this Indian speciality makes a very refreshing dessert. Remove from the freezer 10 minutes before serving to allow it to soften and give the full flavour time to develop.

INGREDIENTS

900g/2lb/5 cups mango pulp
2.5ml/¹/2 tsp lemon juice
grated rind of 1 orange and 1 lemon
4 egg whites
50g/2oz/¹/4 cup caster sugar
120ml/4fl oz/¹/2 cup low-fat Greek yogurt
50g/2oz/¹/2 cup icing sugar

SERVES 4

1 In a large, chilled bowl that can safely be used in the freezer, mix half of the mango pulp with the lemon juice and the grated citrus rind.

NUTRITIONAL NOTES	
Per portion:	
Energy	259Kcals/1090kJ
Fat, total	1.7g
Saturated fat	0.79g
Cholesterol	1.8mg
Fibre	5.9g

2 Whisk the egg whites in a grease-free bowl until soft peaks form, then fold into the mango mixture, with the caster sugar. Cover and freeze for at least 1 hour.

3 Remove the sorbet from the freezer and beat again. Transfer to an ice-cream container, and freeze until solid.

4 Lightly whisk the yogurt with the icing sugar and the remaining mango pulp. Spoon into a bowl and chill for 24 hours. Scoop out individual servings of sorbet and cover each with mango sauce.

LYCHEE AND ELDERFLOWER SORBET

The flavour of elderflowers is famous for bringing out the essence of gooseberries, but what is
less well known is how wonderfully it complements lychees.

INGREDIENTS
175g/6oz/³/4 cup caster sugar
400ml/14fl oz/1²/3 cups water
*500g/1¹/4 lb fresh lychees, peeled
and stoned*
15ml/1 tbsp undiluted elderflower cordial
dessert biscuits, to serve (optional)

SERVES 4

NUTRITIONAL NOTES
Per portion:

Energy	249Kcals/1058kJ
Fat, total	0.1g
Saturated fat	0g
Cholesterol	0mg
Fibre	0.9g

1 Heat the sugar and water until the
sugar has dissolved. Then boil for
5 minutes and add the lychees. Lower the
heat and simmer for 7 minutes. Remove
from the heat and allow to cool.

2 Purée the fruit and syrup. Place a sieve
over a bowl and pour the purée into it.
Press through with a spoon.

3 Stir the elderflower cordial into the
strained purée, then pour the mixture
into a container that is suitable for the
freezer. Freeze for approximately 2 hours,
until ice crystals start to form around
the edges.

4 Remove the sorbet from the freezer
and process briefly in a food processor
or blender to break up the crystals.
Repeat this process twice more, then
freeze until firm.

5 Transfer to the fridge for 10 minutes to
soften slightly before serving in scoops.
Crisp dessert biscuits can be served with
the sorbet, but aren't really necessary. If
you do serve them, remember that they
will increase the fat content of the dessert.

PLUM AND PORT SORBET

Rather a grown-up sorbet, this one, but you could use still red grape juice
instead of port if you prefer.

INGREDIENTS

*900g/2lb ripe red plums, halved
and stoned*
75g/3oz/6 tbsp caster sugar
45ml/3 tbsp water
45ml/3 tbsp ruby port or red wine
crisp, sweet biscuits, to serve (optional)

SERVES 6

1 Put the plums in a pan with the sugar
and water. Stir over a gentle heat until the
sugar has melted, then cover and simmer
gently for about 5 minutes, until the fruit
is soft.

2 Tip into a food processor and purée
until smooth, then stir in the port or wine.
Cool completely, then tip into a container
that can safely be used in the freezer and
freeze until firm around the edges.

3 Spoon into the food processor and
process until smooth. Return to the
freezer and freeze until solid.

4 Soften slightly at room temperature
then serve in scoops, with sweet biscuits
if you like, but they will add fat content.

NUTRITIONAL NOTES
Per portion:

Energy	166Kcals/699kJ
Fat, total	0.25g
Saturated fat	0g
Cholesterol	0mg
Fibre	3.75g

RASPBERRY SORBET WITH A SOFT FRUIT GARLAND

—

**This stunning fresh fruit and herb garnish creates a bold border for the scoops of sorbet.
Make the sorbet in an ice-cream maker, if you have one.**

INGREDIENTS
175g/6oz/3/4 cup caster sugar
250ml/8fl oz/1 cup water
*450g/1lb fresh or thawed
frozen raspberries*
strained juice of 1 orange

FOR THE DECORATION
1 bunch mint
*selection of soft fruits, including
strawberries, raspberries, redcurrants
and blueberries*

SERVES 8

1 Heat the caster sugar with the water in a saucepan, until dissolved, stirring occasionally. Bring to the boil, then set aside to cool. Purée the raspberries with the orange juice, then press through a sieve to remove any seeds.

2 Mix the syrup with the puréed raspberries and pour into a suitable container for the freezer. Freeze for 2 hours or until ice crystals form around the edges. Whisk until smooth, then return to the freezer for 4 hours.

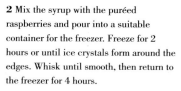

3 About 30 minutes before serving, transfer the sorbet to the fridge to soften slightly. Place a large sprig of mint on the rim of a serving plate, then build up a garland, using more sprigs.

4 Leaving on the leaves, cut the strawberries in half. Arrange on the mint with the other fruit. Place the fruits at different angles and link the leaves with strings of redcurrants. Place scoops of sorbet in the centre.

NUTRITIONAL NOTES
Per portion:

Energy	158Kcals/669kJ
Fat, total	0.4g
Saturated fat	0g
Cholesterol	0mg
Fibre	3.4g

BLACKCURRANT SORBET

Blackcurrants make a vibrant and intensely flavoured sorbet. If not serving immediately,
cover the sorbet tightly and freeze it again, for up to 1 week.

INGREDIENTS
100g/3¹/2 oz/scant ¹/2 cup caster sugar
120ml/4fl oz/¹/2 cup water
450g/1lb/4 cups blackcurrants
juice of ¹/2 lemon
15ml/1 tbsp egg white

SERVES 4

1 Mix the sugar and water in a small
saucepan. Heat gently, stirring until the
sugar dissolves, then boil the syrup for
2 minutes. Remove the pan from the heat
and set aside to cool.

2 Remove the blackcurrants from the
stalks by pulling them through the tines
of a fork. Wash thoroughly.

3 In a food processor fitted with the metal
blade, process the blackcurrants and
lemon juice until smooth. Alternatively,
chop the blackcurrants coarsely, then add
the lemon juice. Stir in the sugar syrup.

4 Press the purée through a sieve to
remove the seeds.

5 Pour the blackcurrant purée into a non-
metallic dish that can safely be used in
the freezer. Cover the dish with clear film
or a lid and freeze until the sorbet is
nearly firm, but still slushy.

6 Cut the sorbet into pieces and process
in a food processor until smooth. With the
machine running, add the egg white
through the feeder tube and process until
well mixed. Tip the sorbet back into the
dish and freeze until almost firm. Chop
the sorbet again and process until smooth.
Serve immediately.

NUTRITIONAL NOTES	
Per portion:	
Energy	132Kcals/558kJ
Fat, total	0g
Saturated fat	0g
Cholesterol	0mg
Fibre	4.1g

MANGO AND LIME SORBET IN LIME SHELLS

This richly flavoured sorbet looks pretty served in the lime shells, but is also good
served in scoops for a more traditional presentation.

INGREDIENTS
4 large limes
1 ripe mango
7.5ml/1½ tsp powdered gelatine
2 egg whites
15ml/1 tbsp caster sugar
strips of pared lime rind, to decorate

SERVES 4

1 Slice the top and bottom off each lime.
Squeeze out the juice, keeping the shells
intact, then scrape out the shell membrane.

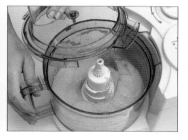

2 Halve, stone, peel and chop the mango.
Purée the flesh in a food processor with
30ml/2 tbsp of the lime juice.

3 Sprinkle the gelatine over 45ml/3 tbsp
of the lime juice in a small heatproof
bowl. Set aside until spongy, then place
the bowl in a pan of hot water, stirring
occasionally until the gelatine has
dissolved. Stir it into the mango mixture.

4 Whisk the egg whites in a grease-free
bowl until they hold soft peaks. Whisk in
the sugar. Fold the egg white mixture
quickly into the mango mixture. Spoon
the sorbet into the lime shells. Any
leftover sorbet can be frozen in small
ramekins.

NUTRITIONAL NOTES
Per portion:

Energy	83Kcals/350kJ
Fat, total	0.4g
Saturated fat	0g
Cholesterol	0mg
Fibre	2.3g

5 Place the filled shells in the freezer
until the sorbet is firm. Overwrap the
shells in clear film. Before serving, allow
the shells to stand at room temperature
for about 10 minutes; decorate them with
knotted strips of pared lime rind.

WATERMELON SORBET

A slice of this refreshing sorbet is the perfect way to cool down on a hot sunny day.
Ensure the watermelon is perfectly ripe when buying.

INGREDIENTS

1/2 small watermelon, about 1kg/2¼ lb
75g/3oz/6 tbsp caster sugar
60ml/4 tbsp unsweetened cranberry
juice or water
30ml/2 tbsp lemon juice
sprigs of fresh mint, to decorate

SERVES 6

1 Cut the watermelon into six equal-size wedges. Scoop out the pink flesh, discarding the seeds but reserving the shell.

2 Select a bowl that is about the same size as the melon and which can safely be used in the freezer. Line it with clear film. Arrange the melon skins in the bowl to re-form the shell, fitting them together snugly so that there are no gaps. Put in the freezer.

3 Mix the sugar and cranberry juice or water in a saucepan and stir over a low heat until the sugar dissolves. Bring to the boil, then lower the heat and simmer for 5 minutes. Leave the sugar syrup to cool.

4 Put the melon flesh and lemon juice in a blender and process to a smooth purée. Stir in the sugar syrup and pour into a freezer-proof container. Freeze for 3–3½ hours, or until slushy.

5 Tip the sorbet into a chilled bowl and whisk to break up the ice crystals. Return to the freezer for another 30 minutes, whisk again, then tip into the melon shell and freeze until solid.

6 Carefully remove the sorbet-filled melon shell from the freezer and turn it upside down. Use a sharp knife to separate the segments, then quickly place them on individual plates. Decorate with mint sprigs and serve.

NUTRITIONAL NOTES

Per portion:

Energy	125Kcals/525kJ
Fat, total	0.52g
Saturated fat	0g
Cholesterol	0mg
Fibre	0.26g

COOK'S TIP

Watermelon seeds make a delicious and nutritious snack if toasted in a moderate oven until brown and hulled to remove the outer shell.

RHUBARB AND ORANGE WATER-ICE

Pretty pink rhubarb, with sweet oranges and honey – the perfect summer ice. Most pink, forced rhubarb is naturally sweet, but if needed, add a little more honey or sugar to taste.

INGREDIENTS
350g/12oz pink rhubarb
1 orange
15ml/1 tbsp clear honey
5ml/1 tsp powdered gelatine
orange slices, to decorate

SERVES 4

NUTRITIONAL NOTES
Per portion:

Energy	38Kcals/158kJ
Fat, total	0.1g
Saturated fat	0g
Cholesterol	0mg
Fibre	2g

1 Trim the rhubarb and slice into 2.5cm/1in lengths. Place the rhubarb in a non-reactive pan.

2 Finely grate the rind from the orange and squeeze out the juice. Add about half the orange juice and the grated rind to the rhubarb in the pan and simmer until the rhubarb is just tender. Stir in the honey.

3 Heat the remaining orange juice and stir in the gelatine to dissolve. Stir it into the rhubarb. Tip the whole mixture into a rigid container that can safely be used in the freezer; freeze for about 2 hours or until slushy.

4 Remove the mixture from the freezer, tip into a bowl and beat well to break up the ice crystals. Return to the freezer until firm. Soften slightly at room temperature before serving in scoops, decorated with orange slices.

ORANGE ICE WITH STRAWBERRIES

Juicy oranges and really ripe strawberries make a flavoursome ice that does not need
any additional sweetening.

INGREDIENTS
6 large juicy oranges
350g/12oz/3 cups ripe strawberries
finely pared strips of orange rind,
to decorate

SERVES 4

NUTRITIONAL NOTES
Per portion:

Energy	124Kcals/518kJ
Fat, total	0.4g
Saturated fat	0g
Cholesterol	0mg
Fibre	5.6g

1 Squeeze the juice from the oranges and
pour into a shallow freezer-proof bowl.
Place the bowl in the freezer. When ice
crystals form around the edge of the
mixture beat the mixture thoroughly.
Repeat this process at 30-minute
intervals over a 4-hour period.

2 Halve the strawberries and arrange
them on a serving plate. Scoop the ice
into serving glasses, decorate with strips
of orange rind and serve immediately with
the strawberries.

COOK'S TIP
The ice will keep for up to 3 weeks in
the freezer. Sweet ruby grapefruits or
deep red blood oranges can be used for
a different flavour and colour.

ICED ORANGES

These tasty little sorbets served in the fruit shell look impressive and are easy to eat – just the
thing for serving at a barbecue or patio picnic.

NUTRITIONAL NOTES

Per portion:

Energy	167Kcals/703kJ
Fat, total	0.3g
Saturated fat	0g
Cholesterol	0mg
Fibre	4.3g

3 Grate the rind of the six remaining
oranges and add this to the syrup.
Squeeze the juice from the oranges, and
from the reserved flesh. There should be
750ml/1¼ pints/3 cups. Top up with
water, if necessary.

4 Stir the orange juice into the syrup,
with the remaining lemon juice and water.
Pour the mixture into a shallow container
that can safely be used in the freezer.
Freeze for 3 hours.

5 Turn the mixture into a bowl, and whisk
to break down the ice crystals. Return
to the freezer container and freeze for
4 hours more, until firm, but not solid.

6 Pack the mixture into the orange shells,
mounding it up, and set the "hats" on top.
Freeze until ready to serve. Just before
serving, make a hole in the top of each
"hat", using a skewer, and push in a bay
leaf as decoration.

INGREDIENTS
150g/5oz/⅔ cup granulated sugar
juice of 1 lemon
200ml/7fl oz/scant 1 cup water
14 oranges
8 fresh bay leaves, to decorate

SERVES 8

1 Put the sugar in a heavy-based pan.
Add half the lemon juice, then pour in
120ml/4fl oz/½ cup of the water. Heat
gently, stirring occasionally, until the
sugar has dissolved, then bring to the
boil, and boil for 2–3 minutes, until the
syrup is clear. Leave to cool.

2 Slice the tops off eight of the oranges,
to make "hats". Scoop out the flesh from
inside each, taking care not to damage
the shell, and set it aside. Put the
empty orange shells and the "hats" on
a baking sheet and place in the freezer
until needed.

COOK'S TIP
Use crumpled foil to keep the shells
upright on the baking sheet.

FRESH ORANGE GRANITA

A granita is like a water ice, but coarser and quite grainy in texture, hence its name.
It makes a refreshing dessert after a rich main course.

INGREDIENTS
4 large oranges
1 large lemon
150g/5oz/²/3 cup granulated sugar
475ml/16fl oz/2 cups water
dessert biscuits, to serve (optional)
pared strips of orange and lemon rind,
to decorate

SERVES 6

1 Thinly pare the orange and lemon rind, avoiding the white pith, and set aside for the decoration. Cut the fruit in half and squeeze the juice into a jug. Set aside.

2 Heat the sugar and water in a heavy-based saucepan, stirring, until the sugar dissolves. Bring to the boil, then boil without stirring, until a syrup forms. Remove the syrup from the heat, add the pieces of orange and lemon rind and shake the pan. Cover and allow to cool.

3 Strain the sugar syrup into a shallow freezer container and add the fruit juice. Stir well to mix, then freeze, uncovered, for about 4 hours until slushy.

COOK'S TIP
To make the decoration, slice extra orange and lemon rind into thin strips. Blanch for 2 minutes, refresh under cold water and dry before use.

---

4 Remove the half-frozen mixture from the freezer and mix with a fork, then return to the freezer and freeze again for 4 hours more or until frozen hard.

5 To serve, turn into a bowl and leave to soften for about 10 minutes, then break up again and pile into long-stemmed glasses. Decorate with the strips of orange and lemon rind. Serve with dessert biscuits, if you like, but remember to take their fat content into account.

NUTRITIONAL NOTES
Per portion:

Energy	139Kcals/589kJ
Fat, total	0.2g
Saturated fat	0g
Cholesterol	0mg
Fibre	1.6g

LEMON GRANITA

**Nothing is more refreshing on a hot summer's day
than a fresh lemon granita.**

INGREDIENTS
475ml/16fl oz/2 cups water
115g/4oz/¹/₂ cup granulated sugar
2 large lemons

SERVES 4

NUTRITIONAL NOTES
Per portion:

Energy	114Kcals/488kJ
Fat, total	0g
Saturated fat	0g
Cholesterol	0mg
Fibre	0g

1 In a large saucepan, heat the water and sugar together over a low heat until the sugar dissolves. Bring to the boil, stirring occasionally. Remove from the heat and allow to cool.

2 Grate the rind from one lemon, then squeeze the juice from both. Stir the grated rind and juice into the sugar syrup. Place it in a shallow container or freezer tray, and freeze until solid.

3 Plunge the bottom of the frozen container or tray in very hot water for a few seconds. Turn the frozen mixture out, and chop it into large chunks.

4 Place the mixture in a food processor fitted with metal blades, and process until it forms small crystals. Spoon into serving glasses.

COFFEE GRANITA

**A granita is a cross between a frozen drink and a flavoured ice, and can be made at home with
the help of a food processor. The consistency should be slushy, not solid.**

INGREDIENTS
475ml/16fl oz/2 cups water
115g/4oz/¹/₂ cup granulated sugar
*250ml/8fl oz/1 cup very strong espresso
coffee, cooled*

SERVES 4

1 Heat the water and sugar together gently until the sugar dissolves. Bring to the boil, stirring occasionally. Remove from the heat and allow to cool.

2 Stir the coffee and sugar syrup together. Place it in a container and freeze until solid. Plunge the bottom of the frozen container or tray in very hot water. Turn the mixture out, and chop into chunks.

3 Place the mixture in a food processor fitted with metal blades, and process until it forms small crystals. Spoon into tall glasses and serve.

NUTRITIONAL NOTES
Per portion:

Energy	115Kcals/488kJ
Fat, total	0g
Saturated fat	0g
Cholesterol	0mg
Fibre	0g

COOK'S TIP
If you do not want to serve the granita immediately, pour the processed mixture back into a shallow container and freeze again. Allow to thaw for a few minutes before serving.

INDEX

NOTES

NOTES

NOTES

NOTES

NOTES

NOTES

NOTES

NOTES